P9-EMO-668

11,002
things to be
miserable
about.

11,002
things
to be
miserable
about.

The Satirical
Not-So-Happy Book

LIA ROMEO and NICK ROMEO

ABRAMS IMAGE | NEW YORK

This book is a parody and has not been prepared, approved, or authorized by the creator of *14,000 Things to be Happy About* or their representatives

Editor: David Cashion
Designers: Galen Smith and Liam Flanagan
Production Manager: Jacquie Poirier

Library of Congress Cataloging-in-Publication Data:

 11,002 things to be miserable about : the satirical not-so-happy book /
by Lia Romeo and Nick Romeo.
   p. cm.
 ISBN 978-0-8109-8363-2
 1. Happiness—Humor. I. Romeo, Nick. II. Title. III. Title: Eleven
thousand two things to be miserable about.
 PN6231.H35R66 2009
 818'.5402—dc22

                          2008031407

Copyright © 2009 Lia Romeo and Nick Romeo

Published in 2009 by Abrams Image, an imprint of Harry N. Abrams,
Inc. All rights reserved. No portion of this book may be reproduced,
stored in a retrieval system, or transmitted in any form or by any
means, mechanical, electronic, photocopying, recording, or otherwise, without written permission from the publisher.

Printed and bound in China
10 9 8 7 6 5 4 3 2 1

Abrams Image books are available at special discounts when purchased in quantity for premiums and promotions as well as fundraising or educational use. Special editions can also be created to speci-
fication. For details, contact specialmarkets@hnabooks.com or the
address below.

HNA ▮▮▮▮▮
harry n. abrams, inc.
a subsidiary of La Martinière Groupe

115 West 18th Street
New York, NY 10011
www.hnabooks.com

To our parents, who made
all the misery possible

INTRODUCTION

Several years ago, a friend passed along a copy of a book called *14,000 Things to Be Happy About*. This cheerful little book is a stream-of-consciousness list of life's small joys, the things that make it worth waking up in the morning, that make us appreciate the beauty in the world and feel glad to be alive.

But what about life's small miseries: the things that make us think about jumping off tall buildings and make us wonder if life is really worth living after all?

No matter how hard we try to convince ourselves that life is a bowl of cherries, the truth is most of the cherries are sour and life basically sucks. And we decided it was time somebody wrote a book about it. (Not that life is always terrible; sometimes the desire to jump off tall buildings subsides and we're satisfied with silent weeping.)

And so, we present *11,002 Things to Be Miserable About*, a stream-of-consciousness list of all the reasons why it's *not* really worth waking up in the morning. *11,002 Things to Be Miserable About* is a much-needed antidote to our culture of raging optimism—greeting cards, self-help books, and all the other ineffective ways we try to make ourselves feel better about existence.

From death and taxes to rhinoviruses, butt acne, and the Hindenburg disaster, *11,002 Things to Be Miserable About* is a book that will make you laugh, cry, and contemplate self-mutilation. Happy reading!

"We're all gonna die!!!"
—Lenny Bruce

Death
Life
Hitler
Erectile dysfunction
Hemorrhoids
Used car salesmen
Your face
Spam (the e-mail)
Spam (the processed meat product)
Vomiting
Blind dates with ugly people
Getting old
Dying young
Victims of lead-based paint
Fake English accents
February
Global warming
Red wine hangovers
The passage of time
Broken condoms
Dead puppies
The working conditions of migrant laborers
Liberal guilt
Your boss
The existence of other people
All the books you will never read before you die
Brutus
Models
The hydrogen bomb
Monday mornings

The orchestra that played as the *Titanic* went
down
Rats
Family gatherings
Michael Jackson's sexual proclivities
Avian flu
Your inner thighs
Mad Cow Disease
Nostril hair
High Rise Cat Syndrome—a surprisingly
common disorder in which urban cats,
well, jump
The Third World
Driver's license photos
Calculus
The subprime mortgage crisis
Punching through a cheap wall
Butt acne
The Mongol invasion
The IRS
The influenza epidemic of 1918
Wild dogs
Laundry
Unrequited love
Unreciprocated oral sex
Bread lines
Vegemite
Lawyers
The airline industry
Gas station bathrooms

Trimethylaminuria—a persistent body odor
    that smells like rotten fish
The Thirty Years War
The Hundred Years War
Male pattern baldness
Imitation crabmeat
David Hasselhoff
The air quality in Beijing
Asparagus
Obesity
The impossibility of ever really knowing
    another person
The Spanish Inquisition
The Donner Party
Sweat
Bedbugs
Having to hear about other people's babies
High heels
Alarm clocks
Exploding manhole covers
Republicans
Democrats
Memoirs by people who are boring
Memoirs by people who are more interesting
    than you
Strychnine
Student loans
Untreated sewage
The final episode of *The Sopranos*
Carbon monoxide poisoning

Your fortieth birthday
Grain alcohol
The Hilton sisters
TV dinners eaten alone
Bifocals
Credit card debt
The day after Christmas
Toxic mold
Jock itch
Idi Amin—a brutal Ugandan dictator
Birds that fly into windows and die
Identity theft
Polyester
Chlamydia
Your childhood
Rhinestone sunglasses
Double chins
Milli Vanilli
The need for health inspectors
Night blindness
Mange
Running into your ex on your way to the gym
Sex after sixty
Cannibalism
Your children criticizing your cooking
Prostate enlargement
Commercials about prostate enlargement
Existential nausea
Actual nausea
Nuclear war

Drilling in polar bear habitats
Oedipus
Nasal irrigation
Mosquito-borne diseases
Olestra
Computer crashes
The bubonic plague
Static cling
Blocks full of ugly office buildings
Suburban backyards that supply their owner's
	sense of self-worth
Being unable to escape an inane conversation
Dropping your fork more than once
The verb "fetishize"
Men who pose for pictures with their cars
Rich people with a veneer of culture
Rich people without a veneer of culture
Logging
Standardized tests
Pus
Literary criticism
Lethal injection
Flushing the toilet, which can spray particles
	of fecal matter up to twenty feet
Playboy bunnies
Rabid dogs
Salmonella
Scoliosis
Flossing
Alien abduction

Dandruff
Colonoscopies
Wine in a box
Unplanned pregnancies
Secondhand smoke
Yeast infections
Commercials about yeast infections
Dropping off dry cleaning
The global economy
Children who want to be cashiers when they
    grow up
Fake gardens in office buildings
Rodent feces
Computer viruses
The fall of Rome
Dramatic miniseries about the fall of Rome
Dentures
Running into old friends you would have
    preferred never to see again
Asbestos
Pesticides
Broccoli
NORAD
Disco
Boils
People who order expensive things when they
    know you're paying
Tapeworms
Men with Napoleon complexes
Anorexia

Cellulite
Pigeons
West Nile Virus
Lice
Dust mites, which make up one-third of the
    weight of a six-year-old pillow
Aerobics
Piranhas
Guar gum
Spontaneous human combustion
Shoulder pads
Acid rain
Tsetse flies
The Riddler
High school orchestra concerts
Styrofoam
Ugly bridesmaids' dresses
Ugly bridesmaids
Electrocution
Fake silver rings that turn your fingers green
Alphabetical organization
Totalitarianism
Artificial grape flavoring
Roadkill
Minivans
Smallpox
Freud
Critics
Investment bankers
The nonexistence of mermaids

The abduction of Helen of Troy
High blood pressure
Tuna noodle casserole
Receiving fund-raising calls during dinner
European men in Speedos
Spiro Agnew
Conjunctivitis
The increasing rates of childhood allergies
Losing your virginity to the wrong person
Seabirds strangled by six-pack rings
Benedict Arnold
Velociraptors
The meatpacking industry
The meatpacking district
Ruddy-cheeked heroines in Victorian novels
Getting invited to your ex's wedding
Library fines
The weak dollar
Shark attacks
Gorgeous weather in Florida when you're
    not there
Other people kissing
Ashlee Simpson
The Godfather: Part III
Forgetting to change your underwear
Remembering to change your underwear,
    then realizing none of your other
    underwear is clean
Hangnails
Scrapple

Back hair
In-laws
The extinction of the dodo bird
Crack
Vanilla Ice
Tropical resorts in desperately poor countries
Keeping up with the Joneses
The smell of subway stations
Pet psychics
The Great Depression
Gas prices
The assassination of Dr. Martin Luther King, Jr.
People who refer to all Latinos as "Mexicans"
Checking your work e-mail from home
Credit card offers
Dentists
Hairy toes
High school Shakespeare productions
Genital warts
Being put on hold
Dogs wearing sweaters
Sausages in a can
The fact that you are no longer seventeen
Rabies
$800 ergonomic chairs and your inability to
    afford one
Hope
Cryogenics
The Crusades
Gentrification

Thai prisons

Poodles

Emo

The Energizer Bunny

Your best friend losing twenty pounds

Belly button lint

Not knowing how to change a tire

Scorpions

The fact that Scandinavia has a higher rate of
English literacy than the United States

Waiting in line

Necrophilia

Being awake at 4 A.M.

Appendicitis

Litigation

Speed bumps

People who actually pursue their childhood
dreams

Getting poked in the eye with somebody's
umbrella

Store clerks that ignore you while they talk on
the phone

Daylight saving time

Cold grease

People who put nonrecyclables in recycle bins

People who put recyclables in trash cans

Arthritis

The Jonestown cult suicides

Running out of toilet paper

School lunch

Pets that are accidentally left to die in hot cars
Pets that are left to die in hot cars on purpose
Insurance companies
Dental fluorosis
Jingoism
Studies that show that the average father
    spends less than thirty minutes a week
    talking to his children
The Malthusian catastrophe—a predicted
    return to subsistence living due to
    population growth outpacing agricultural
    production
People who blog about their personal lives
The stomach flu
Sixteen-year-olds with expensive cars
Having to swipe your own credit card at the
    grocery store
Pompeii
Children who misbehave in restaurants
Fender benders
Finding out that your lover is gay (when
    you're not)
Finding out that your lover is straight (when
    you're not)
Radiation
The death of Elvis
Vending machines that don't work, but take
    your money anyway
Leg cramps
The Macarena

Bad pickup lines
Alligators in the sewer system
Inside jokes that you don't understand
Futility
Hollywood endings
Coupons that expire before you remember to use them
Hair in the shower drain
The eight spiders, on average, that you eat each year in your sleep
Chlorofluorocarbons
Britney Spears' kids
Your bank account balance
Noiseless choking
Small talk
Rotting elk carcasses
Laughter
Sunlight
People who hit their children on the subway
Original sin
The fact that the French get six weeks of paid vacation annually
The improbability of having sex with attractive strangers
Times Square at rush hour
Tourists who spend five minutes looking at each monument
Public housing in East Berlin in the 1970s
The distributions of the world's resources
Twilight

Bad liars
Good liars
The use of lingerie to revitalize failing
    marriages
Birds that shit on you
The pillage of valuable antiquities by English
    gentlemen
Complaining
The heat death of the universe
The end of chivalry
Twelve-year-olds who pose as sex goddesses
    on the internet
People who refuse to admit they're gay
The failure of the world to acknowledge your
    genius
Expectations of reciprocity
Self-pity
Mozart's premature death at thirty-five
Nepotism that doesn't benefit you
Autumn
Reading Beckett when you're depressed
People who pretend to listen while they wait
    to speak
Children who still believe in Santa Claus
Self-indulgence
Self-restraint
Your grandparents' recollections of youthful
    hopes and passions
Scalping
Militant vegetarians

The destruction of the library of Alexandria
The lengthening of shadows in the evening
Bestiality
The inevitable tyranny of social institutions
Clouds
Waiters with delusions of grandeur
Actors
The impossibility of saying just what you mean
Aporia
Playground taunts
Wagnerian sopranos
Your stomach
Unexamined lives
Closely examined lives
Retailers of copy machines
Having to work late
Kilts
Red-bearded men who like killing babies
The average American attention span
Judas
Lower back pain
Fire alarms when there's no fire
Fire alarms when there is a fire
America
Watching Natalie Portman movies with your wife
Saggy breasts
Interminable Oscar broadcasts
MFA programs in creative writing
Claudius
Sylvia Plath and ovens

The death of Socrates
Evolutionary explanations of love
Slow postal workers
Beethoven's deafness
Eye contact with mountain lions
Facing-page translations of Shakespeare into
    modern English
Marriage
Divorce
The obscurity of Alfred Russel Wallace,
    cofounder of the theory of natural selection
Imperfect bladder control
Public beheadings
Fraternities
An ammonia-scented body odor, which is a
    sign of liver disease
People majoring in business
Deriving pleasure from the misfortunes of
    others
Transparent attempts at flattery
Impalement
False pleasantries
Colonialism in Africa
Mean people
Sprawling slums of corrugated tin shacks
The terror felt by children in the dark
Coitus interruptus
Myths in which parents unknowingly
    consume their children in stewed form
Knowing allusions to James Joyce

Sibling rivalry
Blood-drenched dynastic succession struggles
Euphemisms
People who speak loudly in public places
Arranged marriages
The Second Coming
Industrial waste
The sinking of Venice
Pacifists
Determination
Tired waitresses
Counting calories
Richard Simmons
The Penguin
Airborne pathogens
Custody battles
King Lear
Manual labor
The British spelling of "colour"
Compassion
Temperatures at which your face hurts
Slurping noises
Nihilism
Death in the afternoon
Misquotations from the Greek
Being born
Rejection
The doctrine of predestination
Funding for the humanities
The battle of Wounded Knee

Freezing to death in the gutter
Carbohydrates
Siberia
Homes that lack indoor plumbing
Graves, worms and epitaphs
Anthropomorphism
Overly quaint pastry shops
The effects of ethanol on car engines
Custer's last stand
Cotillions
Second marriages
Love
Liposuction
Sarcophagi
Puppet theater
Saying "vagina" in a nonmedical context
Verdi's *Requiem*
The smell of feet in the summer
Landed gentry
Anchovies
Shotgun weddings
The clubbing of baby seals
Wives of sailors lost at sea
Mediocrity
Intestinal parasites
Scientologists who claim to be persecuted
The noses of former boxers
Cleaning products that cause cancer
The Cobra Kai
Theatrical political protests

Jargon
Cauliflower
Hemorrhagic strokes
Countries you've never visited and never will
Sharing toothbrushes
Daytime television
Bureaucracy
Bad credit
Property taxes
Propaganda that makes people go to war and die
Self-expression
Chapped lips
Megalomania
The Gaza Strip
Studies showing that office workers are
    interrupted every three minutes, and take
    twenty-three minutes to get back on task
Open-mic night at the local comedy club
Love letters from people you don't love
    anymore
Cyanide
Psychosis
The assassination of John Lennon
Getting struck by lightning
Migraines
Root canals
Hip replacements
Pedophilia
Not winning the lottery
The vastness of the sea

Commuting

"Television legs"—blood clots as a result of
   watching TV for too long

Dead flowers

The apocalypse

The Dow Jones Industrial Average

Cosmetics tested on rabbits

Midlife crises

Divas

Graduate students

The fact that you are reading this book

People who let their dogs lick their ice cream
   cones

Flogging

Hydrochloric acid

Dehydration

Hyperhydration

Sophomore slump

Multidrug-resistant tuberculosis

Expired airline miles

Coronary artery calcification

Vacuuming

Bear markets

Bear attacks

Bear Stearns

"Bennifer"—the brief and highly publicized
   union of Ben Affleck and Jennifer Lopez

Ethics

Raw beef

The writers' strike

Alex Mitchell, an English bricklayer who
      suffered a fatal heart attack from laughing
      too hard while watching *The Goodies*
Dating advice from your grandmother
Public urination
Botulism
Cholera
Hypertension
Taking out the trash
People who actually think that the glass is
      half full
Getting stood up
Getting stood up because your date is dead
Erosion
Fight-or-flight hormones
Getting honked at (by geese)
Getting honked at (by motorists)
Honorable mention
Cleaning the bathroom
Moldy sponges
Lack of closet space
Inflammation
The smell of nail polish remover
Rotten vegetables
Peeling paint
Unibrows
Unabombers
Magazine articles that tell you your flaws are
      beautiful
Christmas sweaters

The fact that a desk has four hundred times
    more bacteria than a toilet
Highly effective people
January 24—National Compliment Day
Terror and pity
Toenails
The eruption of Mount St. Helens
Panty thieves
Arson
Mexican Jumping Death Spiders
Irritable bowel syndrome
Tension headaches
Your pants size
Polio
Dysthymia—a chronic depressive disorder
Leaving the lights on just to increase your
    roommate's electricity bill
Women who don't realize they're pregnant
    until their water breaks
Dogs with banal human names
The right to bear arms
Girls who think any guy who's not interested
    in them must have a disorder, probably
    Asperger's Syndrome
Girls who think any guy who's not interested
    in them must be gay
Huge warehouses of expired products that
    were never opened
Bus drivers who are a bit too happy to see the
    children after school

Waiters who ramble on about their lives
Broken dress straps
Teenagers discovering the wine cellar
Painfully vigorous hair brushing
Having a third job
Working at a restaurant that has one CD on
continual loop
Unsentimental estimates of how many years
people have left to live
Designer garbage cans
People too busy to have lunch because of
back-to-back meetings with their interior
decorator and life coach
Couples who simultaneously talk on their cell
phones
The moth-infested lace of antique wedding
dresses
Boring relatives from middle America
Accidentally printing a hundred-page document
when you meant to print just one page
Brussels sprouts
Vacations ruined by the children you
shouldn't have had
Automatically rejecting unfamiliar ideas
Seven-year-old boys forced to have phone
conversations with distant relatives
The guillotine
Pigs' feet
Mercury levels in tuna
Cellulose

Getting the middle seat on an airplane
The decline of the rainforests
Your job
Pneumonia
Bullies who stuff people in trash cans
Combination Christmas and birthday presents
Inequity
Soy bacon
Ugly hats
Not getting a holiday bonus
Hairstyles in the '80s
Hairstyles today that look like hairstyles in
    the '80s
People who answer their cell phones in movie
    theaters
The huddled masses yearning to be free
Gingivitis
Gossip
Elderly parents
Chairman Mao
Tax breaks for wealthy people
Working on Sundays
Not knowing which fork to use
Cuckoos
Cuckolds
Mephistopheles
Parallel parking
Monsters under the bed
Forgetting other people's names
Other people forgetting your name

The Peloponnesian War
Restaurants that charge for bread
Slavery
Typhoid
Radon
Trying to get a taxi when it's raining
Men wearing toupees
Capitalism
Communism
Macramé
Brecht
The unlikelihood of your ever attending the
    Academy Awards
The electric chair
Inadequate security measures at nuclear
    power plants
Syringes on the beach
Dust
Middle school band concerts
Cheap gin
Having to sit in the front row at the movies
People who don't wear deodorant
Alcohol poisoning
Unbearably loud music in trendy restaurants
Tear gas
Jeffrey Dahmer
Flat beer
Cold-hearted snakes
The fact that it's illegal to dance in most New
    York City bars

The Berlin Wall
People who misspell your name
People who mispronounce your name
Japanese encephalitis
Car accidents
Bad poetry
Shock and awe
Face lifts
Solitude
Company
Jacobean revenge tragedies
Sympathy cards
Week-old lasagna
Heroin
Elevator music
Game shows
Philistines
Elitists
Ambition
Jihad
Dirty dishes
Winter weight
The ten endless minutes between 4:50 P.M.
    and 5 P.M.
Middle age
The Middle Ages
Mortgage payments
Gift certificates to stores you hate
Skin cancer
Psoriasis

Anyone who puts Baby in a corner
Women with mustaches
Satan
Frozen fish sticks
Eating lunch at your desk
Fat people sitting by you on airplanes
Food poisoning
The carcinogenic potential of silicone breast
     implants
Death by hanging
Student poetry
Bad movie adaptations of good books
The ozone layer
Crystal meth
Benzene
Bad hair days
Minor chords
Mortality
Senior citizens gambling away their life
     savings at casinos
The difficulty of reading in the bathtub
Letters marked RETURN TO SENDER
Pens running out of ink
Split ends
The cancellation of *Arrested Development*
Inflation
People who don't respond to Evites
Man's inhumanity to man
Turbulence on airplanes
Road rage

'Roid rage
Bad jokes
Leftovers
Exhaustion
Exhaust
Worms
Giardia
Heartburn
Clumpy mascara
Infidelity
Orthopedic shoes
Madness
Malapropisms
Clichés
Toadies
Sitcom laugh tracks
Failure
Rusty nails
Yellow fever
Agony
Hairnets
Bruises
Eternity
Valentine's Day
Minimum wage jobs
Sarcasm
MRSA—a virulent skin infection
Premature ejaculation
Your carbon footprint
The nonexistence of unicorns

Freezing rain
Preteens getting pedicures
Barbie
Bulimia
Pop quizzes
Sloppy Joes
Out-of-ink pens
Downer cows
Punching the clock
Spies
Bad movies about spies
Anarchy
The McCarthy era
Dogs that fit in purses
People wearing too-tight clothing
Brain damage
Chipped nail polish
Airline meals
Airlines that don't serve meals
The Japanese zoo animals that starved to
    death during World War II
Decay
Being "just friends"
The draft
Biological warfare
Dead insects floating in swimming pools
Dead insects floating in drinks
Popped balloons
Heavy suitcases
Getting lost in the desert

Designer clothing you can't afford
Sweaty socks
Getting spaghetti sauce on your white shirt
Slums
Forgetting your umbrella when it rains
The explosion of the space shuttle *Challenger*
Bubble-gum-flavored ice cream
Getting your foot stuck in the railroad tracks
   as a train approaches
Scenes in movies about getting your foot
   stuck in the railroad tracks as a train
   approaches
Quiet desperation
Noisy desperation
The extinction of the dinosaurs
The Battle of Gettysburg
The possibility that there is no God
Going home for the holidays
Not going home for the holidays
Monosodium glutamate
Performing monkeys
Disconnected phone calls
Love songs
Braces
Broken bones
Floods
Jet lag
Poorly behaved children
Inferior meals at expensive restaurants
Garage bands

Serial
rapists

Surgeon general's warnings
Forgetting to water your plants
Finding your ex's clothes in your closet
Forest fires
High school reunions
Being wrong
Pol Pot—a ruthless Cambodian dictator
Yellow No. 5
Getting your wisdom teeth out
Dogs that shit in the house
Children that shit in the house
Mistakes
Perverts
Muffin top
Realizing you love someone too late
Realizing you don't love someone too late
Public floggings
The Iron Curtain
Misspelled words
People who talk on their cell phones while
    driving
Ants
The Vietnam War
Feet in need of pedicures
Crime
Not getting a second chance
Trying to sleep on a train
Diet books
Birds sucked into jet engines
Foot fungus

Ear wax
Smiley faces
Ivan the Terrible
Beauty trends
Blisters
Canine diarrhea
Blue laws
Blue eye shadow
Studies showing that the average American
    spends 2.5 hours a day watching TV
Gangrene
The winter of the soul
The gag reflex
Terriers
Terrorists
Headgear
Airplane toilets
The Lawrence Welk Show
Bad polka bands
Good polka bands
Sewage overflows
"La Vie en Rose"
Love scenes in movies featuring "La Vie
    en Rose"
Welts
Bingo
Tasks that expand to fill the time allotted
    to them
The melting polar ice cap
Nightcaps

Nose hair
Needles
Prescription drug abuse
Nonprescription drug abuse
The word "va-jay-jay"
Rumors
The smell of burning rubber
Prostitution
Being "whipped"
Being whipped
Crocodile tears
The unlikelihood of attaining Nirvana
Falling asleep during business meetings
Ashtrays
Soggy napkins
Red wine stains on teeth
Pestilence
Celebrities who claim to have been awkward
    in high school
Fashion victims
Cleaning the toilet
Not cleaning the toilet
Jumpsuits
High school musicals
High School Musical
Gargamel the sorcerer
Tom Cruise
Women who shouldn't wear miniskirts, but do
Women who should wear miniskirts, but don't
Losing a perfect game on the last pitch

Elvis impersonators
Broken glass
Dry skin
Oily skin
Combination skin
Caffeine-free Diet Coke
Distant relatives who expect wedding gifts
Slush falling on your head
Nonfat cream cheese
Bryan Adams
Water bugs
Endangered species
Premature babies
Fake smiles
Potholes
Colic
Kissing someone who's just eaten onions
Stew
Mud huts
Used tissues
Lipstick stains
Tenement housing
Neuroses
Pharmaceutical companies
Racism
Manslaughter
The plight of Tibet
Teenage suicide
Sandstorms
Recession

Bridezillas
Fast food
Cyber-bullies
The cabbage soup diet
Cholesterol
Coal
Ham-handed public policy
Tainted food supplies
Subways at rush hour
Insufficient legroom
Aging
Being "big-boned"
Cold weather in April
Foreclosure
Gnats
Oral herpes
Genital herpes
Wedgies
Homophobia
Saddam Hussein
Inferior quality control
The lack of universal health insurance
Jocks
Jockstraps
Being kicked in the shins
Michael Vick
Plastic bags
Incest
Parties you want to attend but can't
Parties you don't want to attend but have to

Dirty hair
Networking
Optimism
Wrath
Envy
Greed
Gluttony
Lust
Sloth
Pride
Overtime losses
Red Sox fans
Yankees fans
Mason Gross School of the Arts
Tendonitis
Gale-force winds
Ghosts
Menstruation
Celebrities who get engaged after they've
    known each other two weeks
Heart disease
Stuffing envelopes
Temper tantrums
Banned books
Break dancing
Reality TV rejects
The StairMaster
Watching the weather forecast for fun
Getting nervous before doctor's appointments
Moldy bread

Spraining your ankle
Snoring
People who talk too much
People who talk too little
The New Jersey Turnpike
Maniacs
Therapy
Flat tires
Filth
The credit crisis
Your inability to understand the credit crisis
Self-criticism
Genetically modified food products
Glowing reviews of restaurants you can't afford
Counterfeiting
Forgetting to save your work
Fur
Five-legged cows
Three-legged dogs
One-legged people
Children playing in puddles of blood
The numbing influence of time
Staying home alone on New Year's Eve
Smack
Deception
People who have no sense of irony
New York cocktail parties
People who get tattoos of Chinese characters
    but don't know what they mean
March

Brake failure
Feeling like a minor character in the movie of
    somebody else's life
Getting chalk all over yourself
The Real World
The real world
Excess verbiage
Unwanted puppies put in sacks and drowned
Sexual harassment
Ordinary people
Getting pulled over for going five miles per
    hour above the speed limit
Torts
Castration
Military spending
Piece work
The French and Indian War
Alcoholism
The decline of newspapers
Human rights violations
Cold coffee
Misunderstandings
The death of Steve Irwin
The lack of arts funding
Drunk driving
Rhinoceroses getting raped by elephants
    (yes, this actually happens)
Getting pulled over for running a yellow light
Apartment hunting in Manhattan
The smell of burning garbage

Hurricanes
Ugly Americans
Mentally challenged cops
Failing to disguise your hangover in front of
    your boss
Getting a call from your mom while you're
    having sex
Internet porn pop-ups
Loud farts during business meetings
Forgetting everything you learned at school
    over the summer
People who hang fake testicles on their trucks
Trying to ride through a drive-thru on a horse
Ulterior motives
Secret societies you don't belong to
Broken promises
White shirts with yellow armpit stains
Hibakusha, or Japanese atomic bomb survivors
Depreciation
Teenagers
People who steal stop signs
High school dropouts
Beauty school dropouts
Toxic Shock Syndrome
Virginity
Frivolous lawsuits
Frivolous people
Fifty-year-olds who boast about hangovers
Funeral parlors
Sequels

Prequels
The Cobra Commander
The randomness of the universe
The death of movie stars
The death of celestial stars
Lectures
Gray hair
Bills
Safe-crackers
The popularity of Botox
Spit
Rotten teeth
Marching bands
Miles to go before you sleep
Miners
Layoffs
The cost of health insurance
Standing under the mistletoe and not getting
    kissed
Backpacks
Seasickness
JonBenet Ramsey
Performance anxiety
Innocent bystanders
Eyeglasses
Spilled milk
Getting charged as an accessory
The objectification of women
Eternal damnation
Ink stains

The smell of dog food
The taste of dog food
Lifetime movies
People who believe in astral projection
Getting your foot stepped on by someone
    wearing spike heels
Black shoes with white socks
White shoes with black socks
Intestines
The cost of college tuition
Antidepressants
Self-destructive behavior
The secession of South Carolina
Being "pear-shaped"
Ugly jewelry
Maggots
The possibility that a meteorite will extinguish
    all life on earth
The price of flour
The price of designer handbags
Tearing your ACL in the middle of the sports
    season
Trains at rush hour
Losing cell phone reception at critical moments
Side effects
Construction
Constipation
Wall Street
Landfills
Lab results

Logging
Legal fees
Ex–best friends
Unmarked police cars
Downed power lines
Personal injury lawyers
Magazines that speculate incessantly over
    which celebrities are pregnant
The Secret
Not knowing the Secret
Blemishes
Sitting on a bee
Late night subway service changes
Stuttering
Shredder
Not having any money
Eating too much cotton candy
Feeling guilty about not riding your bike to work
The cost of car insurance
Getting a worm in your apple
Pleather
Bunions
Strikes
Outs
Baby squirrels that fall out of trees and die
Carsickness
Mice in restaurant kitchens
Howling dogs
Howling babies
Pamela Anderson

The Triangle Shirtwaist Factory fire
Losing your iPod
Nonrecreational uses of handcuffs
Drinks with algae
Antigone
Existential despair
Financial planning
Zombies
Conspiracies
Conspiracy theories
Television executives
Tests
Bones
Dogs wearing too many ruffles
Women wearing too many ruffles
Red tape
Pet hair
Lost milk carton tops
Football players with necks the size of most
    people's thighs
Willful ignorance
Overcooked vegetables
The self-conscious use of literary devices
Ostentatiously religious people
Watching other men hit on your wife
People who speak in codes you don't understand
Arachnophobia
Rainbow parties
The nail polish odor associated with diabetes
Old cars that break down all the time

The "annexation" of Texas

The fact that the rise of serial killers coincided with the rise of highways

Running out of stamps when you need to mail something

Getting dumped via e-mail

The recent works of Augusten Burroughs

Knowing when your friend from second grade goes to the grocery store, thanks to Facebook status updates

The sound of nails on a chalkboard

"Artesian spring water" that actually comes from a tap

Children whose parents don't pay attention to them

Children whose parents pay too much attention to them

Apples stuffed with razor blades

Weevils

Brothers who fought on opposite sides during the Civil War

Choosing the lesser of two evils

Choosing the greater of two evils

People who are more capable than you

Getting a bad hand of cards

Your lack of artistic ability

Women with enormous engagement rings

Getting injured in the middle of a marathon you've been training for all year

Rocksteady and Bebop

Wishing your shoes were Italian
Wishing you were Italian
Listening to love songs when your heart's
    been broken
Having the wrong answer
Tennis elbow
People with annoying laughs
Not knowing the future
Paying a lot of money to go to a psychic and
    still not knowing the future
Wolves hunted from airplanes
Married men who don't wear their wedding
    rings
Fake flowers on gravestones
Getting your car stolen
Overhead projectors
Forgetting your password
Liverwurst
Worn gray carpeting
Gum stuck under your desk
Microphones that don't work
Third husbands
The Draft Riots
Babies who stick their fingers in electric
    sockets
Fluorescent lighting
Printers breaking late at night
Toilet humor
Soundtracks
Inactivity

Homicide rates
Ugly curtains
Overly tight jeans
Socks with holes in them
Mengistu Haile Mariam—a genocidal
    Ethiopian dictator
Cheating
Dreaming you're naked in public
Dreaming you're taking a test you forgot to
    study for
Prisoners of war
Dull knives
The lack of new islands to discover
Smelly cutting boards
Getting your period on vacation
Wasps at barbeques
The Gulag
Your subconscious
Chipped baseboards
Rusty can openers
People who rent for their entire lives
Pepper spray
The unlikelihood that the words "Lights!
    Camera! Action!" will ever apply to you
People with fabulous hair
Styrofoam peanuts
Getting lost in a foreign country
Saying something stupid
Getting ink on your hands while reading the
    paper

The cat getting out
Your relationship with your father
Insincerity
TV psychics
Small boys killing ladybugs
Squeaky rocking chairs
Permanent frown lines
Led Zeppelin cover bands
Tarantulas
Infertility
Dirty windows on sunny days
Your lack of heirloom jewelry
Stepmothers
Hysteria
Winos
Homelessness
Bad remakes of classic movies
Slammed doors
Vicious cycles
Putting the car in drive when you meant to put
    it in reverse
When amputation is the best solution
Discovering that you haven't yet hit rock bottom
The Afghan government's protection of the
    opium trade
Easy chairs with rips and tears
Scuffed patent leather shoes
Old girdles
Women with men's names
Men with women's names

Overstuffed closets

Defenestration, or throwing someone out of a window

Huge wads of electrical cords behind old TVs

Lost toothpaste caps

People who try to talk like they're from Jamaica

Posters that keep falling down

Waxing poetic

Waxing unwanted hair

Garbage on the sidewalk

Small children sticking marbles up their noses

Carnivorous plants

Adversity

Advertising

Decapitation

Restoration comedy

MC Hammer

Trying to use your hairdryer abroad and having it blow up in your face because it's the wrong voltage

People who love what they do

People who hate what they do and never stop complaining about it

Kamikaze pilots

The smell of Teen Spirit

Rapidly approaching tornadoes

Stepping in dog shit

Promotions of coworkers

Trying to balance career and family

Failing to balance career and family

Ralph Nader's insistence on repeatedly
    running for president
Buying vegetables and forgetting to eat them
Leaving the oven on
Accidentally setting off your car alarm
Leaving your wallet at home
Your date claiming they left their wallet at home
Cat burglars
Regular burglars
Old maids
Men who don't put down the toilet seat
People who die alone and don't get found until
    their bodies start to smell
Sitting on a tack
The Battle of the Bulge
Urban ghettoes
Preservatives
Stultifying heat
The Panic of 1837
Forgetting to lock your door
Remembering to lock your door, but worrying
    all day that you forgot to
People who blast bad music
Scars
Moles
Squamous cell carcinoma
Hat hair
The whales in need of saving
Bad puns
Teenagers who smoke

Accidentally ingesting rat poison
Intentionally ingesting rat poison
Hyenas
Beelzebub
Farmer's tans
The Patriot Act
Sunglasses at night
Advertising jingles that get stuck in your head
The calories in a serving of macaroni and cheese
Telemarketers
Jehovah's Witnesses
Cults
Drought in Ethiopia
Becoming a statistic
Homeless pets euthanized in overcrowded
    animal shelters
Trying to figure out how much tip to leave at
    restaurants
Not wanting to be part of any club that would
    have you as a member
Machiavelli
AIDS needles
Guys that don't call
Girls that don't answer when you call
Guys that don't answer when you call
Going out to dinner with people who order the
    most expensive thing on the menu, and
    then want to split the bill
The death of James Dean
Foreigners who speak better English than you

Oversights
Limitations
The one that got away
Failing to meet the U.S. RDA of vitamins
Scabs that won't heal
Gael Garcia Bernal's height
The Children's Crusades
Clothes that go out of style the year after you
    buy them
Books devoted to helping women find a husband
Car bombs
Slurry
Embarrassment
Not having a comeback
Having the perfect comeback an hour too late
Cafeteria food
Death row
The end of the world
Soggy cereal
Sleepwalking
Not having any privacy
The unbearable lightness of being
The agony of defeat
Thin ice
The Yakuza
General Sherman's scorched earth policy
Eating an entire roast chicken
Boutiques that go out of business
Hydrogenated fat
Oral fixations

Illegal immigrants working in
  slaughterhouses
Unpaid internships
Getting older but not wiser
Other people's birthdays
Chicago in winter
People who yawn while you're talking
Reading travel magazines about places you
  can't afford to visit
The price of organic food
Contractors
False inferences
Chain restaurants full of kitschy fake Americana
Fundraising
Holy war
Homeland Security
Widows
Widowers
People who track dirt onto your floor
Corporate hatchet men
Homeowners' associations
Termites
Difficult clients
Aftershocks
People who wear face masks to go outside
Additional taxes and fees
A $175 hamburger made with real gold (this
  actually exists)
Coffee snobs
Ill-fitting suits

Alligator attacks
Lindsay Lohan
Big oil
Bad sushi
Actors who think they can sing
The connection between obesity and global
	warming
People who get lung cancer even though
	they've never smoked
Monster truck rallies
Cars with poor gas mileage
The rising unemployment rate
Being overqualified for your job
Being underqualified for your job
Fidel Castro
Humiliation
Waterboarding
Energy bills
First-degree murder
Second-degree murder
Third-degree murder
Roundworms
Overeaters Anonymous
People who are paid for being attractive
Unattractive neighbors who get the mail in
	their underwear
People who sell their kidneys to make rent
People with insatiable cravings for attention
Unrealistic expectations
Disequilibrium

Hurricane Katrina
The federal government's response to
    Hurricane Katrina
Withering self-assessments
Punishments that don't fit the crime
Little boys who want to be assassins when
    they grow up
Overcrowded homeless shelters
Deflated soufflés
Your work/life balance
Diabetic cats
Nannies with advanced degrees
Exterminators
Women who enjoy making men fight over them
Boxers who are killed in the ring
Retinitis pigmentosas—a hereditary condition
    that leads to blindness
The ban on gay marriage
People who give away the endings of movies
Politicians who sleep with prostitutes
Disaster fatigue
Margarine
The banality of evil
Waiting for test results
Scabies
The high levels of potentially toxic chemicals
    found in household pets
Bad stand-up comics
Nonbiodegradable materials
Dissecting rats

Tobacco companies
Radiation leaks
Casualties
Airlines that charge for checked baggage
Hearing your neighbors having sex
The fact that you're more likely to be
    overweight if your friends are overweight
New York City public schools
Budget cuts
Eczema
Antibiotic resistance
Low birth weights
Dowdy clothes
Arrested development
Juntas
Men with too much testosterone
Men without enough testosterone
The Peter Pan mentality
Stop-gap measures
Predictions that oil prices are just going to
    keep going up
Rhinoviruses
The Taliban
Deflation
Soldiers with inadequate body armor
Contaminated toothpaste
The Victorian belief that sex with a virgin was
    a cure for STDs
Jury duty
Formal wear

Lard

Carpooling with annoying coworkers
Not carpooling with annoying coworkers but
    feeling guilty about it
Clutter
Government corruption in New Jersey
Not having a contingency plan
Parents who can't stop offering advice
Disorganization
Competition
Feeling overwhelmed
Untrained workers on mental health hotlines
To-do lists
The Safety Dance
Lima beans
Being hit on at church
Propane tank explosions
Mutants
People who blog about their sex lives
Pathogenic bacteria
Marrying a man with an awful last name
Tainted pet food
Mechanical bulls
Railroad apartments
Your boss finding you on Facebook
Your students finding you on Facebook
The morning after
The D-list
Chronic obstructive pulmonary disease
Iron lungs
Ice storms

Athlete's foot
Hookworm
The Trail of Tears
Egotists
The news
Death traps
People who mispronounce the names of
    foreign cities
The death of Robert Altman
"Toxic jock" behavior
Potentially toxic chemicals found in
    Nalgene bottles
Dweebs
Wasting hours on instant messenger
People who wear chain mail as a fashion
    statement
Televangelists
Bedazzlers
McMansions
Fossil fuels
Serfs
Being thrust into the spotlight
The link between eating red meat and an
    increased risk of colon cancer
The Mafia
Nuclear proliferation
Innocent people who are wrongly convicted
Chemtrails
Orphans
Teenage runaways

Finance charges

Fecal matter coming into contact with meat in slaughterhouses

People who do stupid things for shock value

Bubblegum pop

Fantasizing about people you will never have sex with

Court-ordered community service

Orlando Bloom as an action hero

Fitness magazines that remind you how out of shape you are

Feeding frenzies

Relapses

Trinkets

The fact that the U.S. Air Force accidentally shipped six nuclear-tipped missiles across the country without knowing it

Alcatraz

Malfunctioning toilets

Artillery

Choppy water

Hypochondria

Using a slow internet connection

The smell of hair dye

Cars with no air conditioning

Jealousy

Parents who outlive their children

Raw nerves

Rising beer prices

Buckshot

Getting your hair cut
Swallowing a bitter pill
Having to send a fax when you don't have a
     fax machine
Biblical theme parks
Waxing your bikini line
Not waxing your bikini line
People who have no limbs
The Kennedy curse
Vintage clothes that cost more than new clothes
Denial
Anger
Bargaining
Depression
Acceptance
Wine that's been in the fridge too long
Vendor relations
Rising rates of STDs among senior citizens
Cruise ships illegally dumping hazardous
     wastes into the ocean
Chernobyl
Skinheads
The fact that the average employee has a one-
     in-three chance of being fired
Credit card companies
Debtors' prison
Slave ships
Ghost towns
People with multiple personalities
Megastores

Stagnant wages

Dick Cheney

Trying to figure out how to work your digital camera

Death spirals

Being transferred

Catholic guilt

Gas vapors

Formaldehyde

The link between hair dye and an increased risk of lymphoma

Germs on doorknobs

"Economy-class syndrome"—blood clots in the legs caused by sitting too long in a confined space

Contaminated dirt around construction sites

E. coli

Flatworms

People who sneeze on the salad bar

Stomach cramps

Bad dancers

Pinching pennies

Amnesia

Urine samples

Hand-me-downs

The caste system

Finding out that the light at the end of the tunnel is an oncoming train

Over-limit fees

Universal default

People who get crushed by falling pianos
Mistaken identity
Stagflation
El Niño
Low approval ratings
Disappearing glaciers
Lunges
Squats
The plight of the American South during
    Reconstruction
Skipping dinner to save money for drinks
Coveting thy neighbor's wife
Coveting thy neighbor's salary
Being strip-searched
Ice queens
Dogs eating their own shit
Dogs eating other dogs' shit
Turf wars
Sani Abacha—leader of bloody Nigerian coups
Not being in the mood
Bullet wounds
Mercantilism
Bad eggs
Increasing rates of childhood obesity in
    developing countries
Metallic leggings
Wannabes
The cold shoulder
Maoist rebels
Children with a sense of entitlement

Politicians who try to play up their working-
    class credentials
Post-traumatic stress disorder
Karma
Crane accidents
The disappearance of the early settlers of
    Roanoke Island
The fact that 20 percent of U.S. households
    are without internet access
"Free trials" that automatically enroll you in
    an expensive plan that's difficult to cancel
Favoritism
Hype
Riots
Flabby arms
Leopard print accessories
Banana hammocks
Geometric proofs
Business trips
Hair on the soap
Text-message breakups
Routine
Not liking his friends
Not liking her friends
Workaholics
Deer that get hit by cars
Cars that get hit by deer
Four-hour erections
Prerequisites
Cops who commit suicide

The seven-year itch
Bad investments
Vitamin deficiency
Macular degeneration
Nuclear testing
Naugahyde boots
Immense restaurant portions
Upbeat celebrities battling cancer
International incidents
Not being able to afford a personal trainer
Keeping up appearances
Funerals
The death of Princess Diana
Mystery meat
Finding out what happened on your favorite
    show before you've watched it
Alopecia, or spot baldness
Polluted rivers
Pacemakers
Dubious distinctions
Clay Aiken
Championship horses that break their legs
    and have to be put to death
Middle management
Ted Kennedy's brain tumor
Infectious diseases
Tasers
The smell of chlorine
Wasps
WASPs

Red-eye flights
The War of 1812
Trying to get a mortgage
Righteous indignation
Updating your résumé
Self-promotion
Rituals of manhood that involve being staked
    to a red ant hill
Sounding stupid
Eugenics
People who cancel plans
People who are born with vestigial tails
Men who spend more on hair products than
    most women do
Forgotten biographers of minor statesmen
Drool
Alex Rodriguez's $28 million salary
People who think they can play guitar
Recent reports indicating that NASA
    "marginalized or mischaracterized" global
    warming studies
Accidentally setting your hair on fire
Kidney stones
Brown recluse spiders
Long wedding ceremonies
Sleet
Fashion magazines that make you believe you
    can actually reinvent yourself
Waking up next to someone you don't
    remember going to bed with

Codependency

Ugly ties

PCP

The Hapsburgs and the Hohenzollerns

Lost luggage

People who wear too much perfume

Reverend Jeremiah Wright

Nightmares

Hearing loss

Volcanic activity

Mucus

Lime-flavored Jell-O

Filling out the same information on twenty
different job applications

Deer that eat your flowers

Bleeding Kansas

The death of Yves Saint Laurent

The fact that the FDA inspects only about 1
percent of all U.S. food imports

Men who cheat while their wives are pregnant

People who fake their own deaths for life
insurance money

Studies suggesting a link between cell phone
use and brain cancer

Variety shows

Corey Haim

Desertification

Looking at your high school trophies for
sports you don't play anymore

Swollen lymph nodes

Ashes

Secondhand cars that smell like stale cigarette smoke

The impossibility of ever completely understanding the universe

Monotony

Accidentally running over small animals

Store clerks who stare at you blankly when you ask them a question

Setting off the airport metal detector

Prosthetic limbs

Dental abscesses

Losing an expensive pair of sunglasses

Having a hole in your underwear

Yuppies

Doctors who say "the patient is experiencing unexpected complications" when they mean "the patient is going to die"

Writers who have mastered everything but writing

Bathing in someone else's dirty water

Screenwriters working as telemarketers

Assistants to minor celebrities

Working the late shift at 7-Eleven

People who go to your funeral to make sure you're really dead

Toddlers incapable of being potty trained

Grocery carts that cause car accidents

Hazardous material removers

Websites dedicated to pictures of vomit

Being the before model in the before and after
    picture
Falling in love due to dim lighting
Feeling relieved to learn that your children
    have been kidnapped
People who don't realize that there is more
    than one sexual position
People with abnormal attachments to their
    pets
Countries united by the prospect of lucrative
    foreign wars
Men with Jesus beards
Men whose sexual fantasies come from
    science fiction
People who are greedy at work and greedy in
    bed
People who assume that God is whatever
    gender and ethnicity they are
Living with a hypochondriac
Discovering too late that your boyfriend is a
    sadist
Boat people
Being mistaken for a boy
Being mistaken for a girl
Underfunded museums forced to close
Grocery prices at Whole Foods
Secret police forces
Rattlesnakes
Mutiny
Small children choking on toys

Hummers in suburbia
People who are perpetually trying to find
    themselves
Opportunistic infections
People who win the Darwin Awards
Visa regulations
Quicksand
Brothels
Children who die trying to re-create stunts
    from movies
Paying retail price
Atmospheric radiation
Narcolepsy
The vastness of space
Obsessive-compulsive disorder
Nasty tricks
Red eyes in photographs
Stepfathers
Cheap beer
Getting a crack in your windshield
Talking to yourself out loud in public
Sleeping in your car
Mildew
Wrinkly necks
Dirty glasses
Pep rallies
Recipes that call for obscure ingredients
Trauma wards
The suffering of Job
Bipolar disorder

Wanting to save the world but not knowing how
The Alamo
Booty calls
The Boston Massacre
The possibility that your husband would
    rather have sex with little girls
Beggars
Industrial pollutants
Organic chemistry
Getting evicted
Chain gangs
Road work
Drug dealers
Rehab
The possibility that a snake will make its way
    out of the sewer system and into your
    toilet
Warren S. Jeffs—leader of a controversial
    Mormon polygamist sect
Chronic wasting diseases
Condors with lead poisoning
Lethargy
Yog-Sothoth
Dysmenorrhea
The available job prospects for philosophy majors
Methane
Heteronormativity
The Middle East
Catheters
Drag racing

Fertilizers in the water supply

Snobs

Sodomized polar bears

Environmental groups that waste paper by
sending out junk mail

Wondering whether the person you're with is
the person you ought to marry

Getting hit on at gas stations

Soul patches

Children who asphyxiate themselves with
plastic bags

People who wear the same clothes for several
consecutive days

Cobwebs

Bimbos

Men who like bimbos

Ballyhoo

The bogeyman

Domestic servants

The assassination of Robert F. Kennedy

People who are over thirty and are still being
supported by their parents

Group e-mail lists where people ceaselessly
debate minor points to distract themselves
from the monotony of their lives

Drowning

Senescence

Pirates

Movies of the week

Having the same arguments over and over

Having nothing better to do than watch
    movies of the week
Health risks associated with energy drinks
Hit and run accidents
Unsolved mysteries
Salad that's been in the fridge too long
Eating pizza out of the garbage can
Having a weird name
The extinction of millions of insect species
    due to pollution
The fact that despite the extinction of
    millions of insect species due to pollution,
    cockroaches are doing just fine
Sodium benzoate—a preservative linked to
    cell damage
Missed free throws
Nuclear meltdown
Hepatitis A
Hepatitis B
Hepatitis C
Facebook applications
Jumping through hoops
The sinking of the Andrea Doria
The fact that the U.S. has the highest STD rates
    of any country in the industrialized world
Nicotine
The link between weight gain and
    antidepressants
Blackwater
Perky animated animals

Overweight miniature dogs
Skunks
The difference between life and '80s movies
The near-extinction of California condors
Burnout
Tightrope walkers who fall off their tightropes
    and die
Scheduling conflicts
Scatological humor
Polemicists
Neanderthals
Andrew Lloyd Webber musicals
Plutocratic democracy
Raunch culture
The possibility that overuse of hand sanitizer
    will lead to new strains of antibiotic-
    resistant bacteria
Subway poles
Attachment disorder
Being raped by hyenas
Being in the wrong place at the wrong time
Windows that don't open
Forgetting favors you owe others
Remembering favors you owe others
Forgetting favors others owe you
Scuzzy motels
Melted snowmen
Printing errors
Eulogies for gerbils
Dog breath

Willful misunderstandings
Blaming your parents for the person you've
    become
Nantucket red
Spending your life savings on whores
Hearing your mother say "tits"
Bidets used as drinking fountains
Dead opossums
Ravens blotting out the sunset
Overexposed film
The bends
Swingers
Ungrateful invalids
The heart of darkness
Richard Nixon
Greasy men in overalls
Mustaches
The Milgram Experiment
Neglected grandmothers
Popular culture
Celebrity baby photos sold for millions of
    dollars
Feverish sell-offs on Wall Street
Automobile safety before Ralph Nader
Soap operas
Nazi sympathizers
Heat-seeking missiles
Anhedonia—the inability to experience pleasure
Opponents of miscegenation
Children named after rock stars

Crucifixion

Bad dialogue
Quaaludes
Queasiness
Dozing at dinner parties
Evolutionary dead ends
Sensible shoes
Human refuse
Longing for the womb
Noblesse oblige
Poor vaginal hygiene
Distant thunder
Nearby thunder
Newly discovered diseases
Blacking out
Opportunists
Self-hating short people
Short circuits
Sixty-five-year-olds with Dorothy Hamill
    haircuts
Pitch-correction software that makes people
    who can't sing into pop stars
Strip mall family restaurants
Guilt management seminars
Haikus by seventh graders
Dirty bombs
Dirty bathtubs
Poison oak
Crypts
Being told to obey the Golden Rule
The eighth cup of coffee

The Ringling Bros. and Barnum & Bailey fire
   of 1944
Lakefill
Men who have sex with only virgins
Realizing your order is wrong after the
   delivery man has left
The nonexistence of magic carpets
The assumption that midgets are funny
Third times that are not the charm
Vengeance
People who romanticize victimization
Charles Taylor—accused war criminal and
   former president of Liberia
Children who are molested by priests
Losing your umbrella
Bulging eyes
Civilized predators
Parents who have favorite children
Children who have favorite parents
Psychosomatic symptoms
Grippe
Toothbrushes in toilet bowls
The Charge of the Light Brigade
Ballerinas turned strippers
Not owning a villa in Tuscany
Tomb raiders
Prostate exams
The patriarchy
Mental asylums
Nagasaki

Minor league baseball players who never
   make it to the majors
Rigged elections
Penal colonies
Schools with honor codes that no one follows
The smell of carrion
Dancing on graves
Dilettantism
Museums that steal Greek antiquities from
   innocent farmers
Delighting in perceived superiority
Being judged by your kitchen
Spit valves
Being a finalist but not winning
Chinchillas skinned alive for their fur
People who take one bite out of every piece in
   a box of chocolates
Being asked what your call is regarding
Gratuitous references to Foucault
Elitist cemeteries
The sunk costs error
Children who are accidentally locked in
   refrigerators
Corporate takeovers
Being stabbed to death with a butter knife
People who rip your clothes off when you're
   wearing nice clothes
Class warfare
The Hellmouth
Why God permits suffering

Always blinking in photographs
Electroshock therapy
Turkish soldiers who tossed babies on their
    bayonets in front of their parents
Low ink cartridges
Antiquarianism
Forgotten epiphanies
Deadly nightshade
Schizophrenia
People who inform you about their bodily
    functions
The fact that Russian characters in old movies
    are always named Boris and Natasha
Having the same last name as a famous person
Having the same phone number as a popular
    restaurant
Zoonotic diseases
Drug patents that prevent the production of
    generic versions of lifesaving medicines
Research breakthroughs that come too late
Frontiersmen who had to bury their own wives
Self-diagnosis based on internet research
Syncope—a temporary loss of consciousness
Malnutrition
Stunted growth
Cow-tipping
Allusions you don't understand
Books of lists
Cantaloupe-sized tumors
Painfully tight hugs

Being unable to drink the water in foreign
    countries
Starving dogs
Underfunded hospitals
Guy Fawkes
Nero fiddling while Rome burned
People with family money
Nondisclosure agreements
Apartheid
Shrinking payrolls
Deathwatch beetles
Your neighbor refusing to lend you a cup of
    sugar
Unpronounceable names
Discovering you have siblings
Pubic lice
Trade embargos that result in starvation
Misdirection of public funds
Outdoor showers
Opportunity costs
Testing new drugs on poor people
Skinny legs
"When the evening is spread out against the
    sky like a patient etherized upon a table"
Roads through rainforests
Brood parasitism
Northern latitudes
The Middle Passage
Airborne viruses
Climbing stairs

Haunted houses
Unsterilized needles
The projects
Chaff
The suicide of Ernest Hemingway
Glasses that fog up when you come inside
Feeling guilty about taking your allotted
    vacation days
Nosebleeds
Skeletons
Children whose parents can't afford school
    supplies
Molluscum contagiosum
Vitamin deficiencies
Wearing the same dress as someone else at
    the same party
Tila Tequila
Sole lifts
Machine guns
Bad movie adaptations of *Hamlet*
Celebrity sex tapes
Dead babies
No guts, no glory
Plus-size models who are thinner than normal
    people
Surgical masks
People who dress as Jesus for Halloween
Jokes that aren't funny anymore
Jokes that were never funny to begin with
Grandmothers in bikinis

Miracle diets that don't work
Breath that smells like rotting meat
Chartless deserts
Men who cheat on their wives with their nannies
Succubi
Getting to hell before the devil knows you're
    dead
Liver and onions
Being born to suffer
Training bras
Other people's babies vomiting on you
Toilets in third world countries
Slow-burning fires of hatred
People who club their families to death with
    baseball bats
Mattresses that ruin your back
Teachers who aren't as smart as you
Eating after you've brushed your teeth
Friends who never call
High rollers
Lobotomies
Aging courtesans
Your anaerobic threshold
Drinking wine from plastic cups
The Battle of Thermopylae
The Crimean War
Loneliness
Wagging the dog
"The Rachel" haircut
Malaria net shortages

Mail-order brides
Misleading product testimonials
Soft-core porn
Snapped ligaments
Self-sodomy with broomsticks
Belladonna
Cosseted wives
Cosseted husbands
Dying of exposure
Policemen who fire on protestors
Ceramic angels
Paralysis
Spoiled milk
Suspension of due process
Blood-borne illnesses
Old men delivering pizzas
Hundred-degree nights
Serial womanizers
Vibrating with fear
Costs that outweigh benefits
The Stanford Prison Experiment
In-flight magazines
Aging inmates
Going prematurely gray
Models who aren't dumb
Free radicals
Mariah Carey's outfits
Self-immolation
Dolphins with missiles strapped to their noses
The N word

People who use the euphemism "do it" for sex
The homely and unloved
Campfires that turn into forest fires
Ailing old men in blizzards
Tired journalistic prose
Anal fungus
Congressional graft
Mussolini
Mania
Blaming the victim
Poets who dabble in politics
Politicians who dabble in poetry
Air conditioners that drip on your head when
    you're walking down the sidewalk
Escaping a war-torn nation at a young age on
    a flimsy raft
Children raised by polygamous sects
The Playboy Mansion
The Mexican-American War
Morphine addicts
Imperfect murders
The Red Scare
Betrayed constituencies
Long-lost identical twins
Double-dating with your widowed parent
Hipsters
Hippies
Plagiarism
The Khmer Rouge
Oxide of arsenic

Great orators with throat cancer
Ritalin addiction
Brutal fraternity hazing
Asperger's syndrome
Cardiomyopathy—a disease in which the
    heart muscle becomes weakened
American seamen who were compelled to
    serve in the British navy in 1807
Demonic possession
People who have "the third" or "the fourth"
    after their name
Bad professors with tenure
Fighter jets
Dog funerals
Religious vestments in hot weather
Male escorts
Prison guards
Refugee camps
Downward spirals
The dwindling social networks of the elderly
Visible panty lines
Untalented children of celebrities who
    become famous singers
Wearing braces for decades
Wandering through a dark labyrinth
Ethicists paid to condone the dubious
    decisions of large corporations
Diets described as revolutions
The irrelevance of modern academic philosophy
Fake logs that never burn

Inattentive lifeguards
Horse tripping—a rodeo sport based on
    tripping running horses
Demands presented as requests
Trivial distinctions
DEET—a toxic chemical in mosquito repellent
People who refer to war as an art
Termination of unemployment benefits
Men who eat meat off knives
Red ink
False accusations of rape
Melancholy angels
People who use Febreze as deodorant
The runs
Deaths of salesmen
Whiskey before noon
Novelists imprisoned for their political beliefs
Ethnic cleansing
Chicken jerky cutlets
Plantar fasciitis
Plantar warts
Compulsive paper shredding
Scylla and Charybdis
Special-interest money
Gloom
Pregnancy
FEMA trailers
Paranoia
Illiteracy
Criminal records

Exasperated relatives
Kind-hearted felons
Blistering criticism
Electric bills
Nutraloaf—a food loaf served as punishment
    to unruly American prisoners
The hottest day of the year
The coldest day of the year
Hearing voices
Religions with CEOs
Food stamps
Failed children of prominent parents
Having to smile repeatedly for family
    photographs
Picking up the wrong medication at the
    pharmacy
Hunger strikes
The amount of water used on golf courses
Rationing
Inept shoplifters
Caveats
Proctologists
Acidophilus milk
Water shortages in Florida and California
Vampire bats
Liquid diets
Sugarcoating
Troglodytes
Unanswered prayers
Vomiting on your lover

Getting your knickers in a twist
People who are convinced they're going to
     heaven
Armies destroyed in half an hour
Putrefying shellfish
Trampled flowers
Soggy hotdogs
Going astray in the darkness
Losing your charm
Overworked donkeys
Aging ballparks
Visiting your child on death row
Squeak toys
Armed bandits
Swaziland, the nation with the world's highest
     death rate
Good intentions lost on the way to the
     grocery store
Studies that suggest you're going to die in the
     near future
Photocopies of genitals
Losing a hand to a paper shredder
Intentionally stabbing yourself with a pencil to
     get disability pay
The quality of prose in *TV Guide*
Attributing every hot day to global warming
Scientists at the Environmental Protection
     Agency who fear retaliation from the Bush
     Administration if they speak about their work
Malfunctioning mirror neurons

Prefabricated homes made from war-surplus
	aluminum
The 13,411 golf cart injuries in 2006
Dreary early morning light
Sex with first cousins
Military parades
Having your tongue torn out
Doses strong enough to kill a horse
The red light district
Cloven hoofs
Ticks
Sharpened stakes at the bottom of deep pits
The voracity of oblivion
Fratricide
Sacrificial lambs
Cobalt 60
The weight of the unknown
The fall of the sparrow
Drowsiness caused by eating too much at lunch
Observing meaningless traditions
Prolonged incestuous violation by your father
Men who say "splendid"
Picnicking spectators at Civil War battles
Cockfighting
Disquieting beauty
Sunken galleons
The difference between life and romance novels
Ineffective social workers
Entanglements with cows
Inheriting your grandfather's wardrobe

Lampshades made out of human skin
Dying while waiting for the mail to come
Shirts soaked with blood
Musty wedding dresses
Winchester rifles
Sewing machine accidents
Abysses of regret
Muteness
Exaggerated vows of love
Tipping over backward in your chair
Chasing a greased pig
Specters from the past
Receding hairlines
The Salem witch trials
Soldiers quartered in civilian homes
Colombian assassins
Hiroshima
The misery of goldfish
Undertakers
Forgetting to celebrate Christmas
Identity politics
Terrible expiation
Economy class
Blood sports
Blood diamonds
Your grandfather's penis
Legalized atrocities
Losing a contact lens
The smell of gunpowder
Soldiers who miss killing people

Exploding inner organs
Suburban boredom
Being unable to remember the last time you
    had sex
Forgetting to wear sunscreen at the beach
Guerrilla warfare
Dialysis
Heel pain caused by flip-flops
Hyperhidrosis—abnormally increased
    perspiration
Treating gunshot wounds with prayer
DDT—a toxic pesticide
Corns
Tendinosis
Having a condition that stumps your doctors
Knowledge that is not power
Low blood pressure
Memory decline
Pesticide residues
New Year's resolutions
The London Blitz
Bombardment
Blowing your paycheck
Blowing your boss
Movie stars who appear not to age
Teachers who are mistaken for students
Cremation services
Drug smuggling
Human smuggling
Hidden cop cars

Apartment swaps gone wrong
Colorectal surgery
The link between vaccination and autism
The link between nonvaccination and death
Stool samples
The gall bladder
Meeting your husband's other wife
Ulcers
Income tax
Executives who expense prostitutes to
    corporate accounts
Remote controlled machine guns
Socially acceptable prejudices
Aging beauty queens
Glass ceilings
Zookeepers mauled by tigers
Rationales for murder
World War II–era bombs unearthed in
    European cities
Pets treated with psychoanalysis
Charismatic villains
Moments of reckoning
Oliver Cromwell
Castrating yourself
People who have more Facebook friends
    than you
The primrose path to the everlasting bonfire
Coyotes
Wrecking balls
Making a silk purse out of a sow's ear

Prenuptial agreements
Ash Wednesday
Accidentally sleeping on baby bunnies
Trolling the internet for sex
Lying about your height
Lying about your weight
Lying about your age
Robberies committed with pepper spray
Advertising budgets
Dead Girl Scouts
Wishing you'd had an abortion
Bodies found in rivers
Adolescent eye-rolling
Crimes against nature
Damaged goods
Ears popping on airplanes
Coffin-makers
Lynch mobs
Komodo dragons
Brutalist architecture
Dangerous undertows
The whereabouts of the Holy Grail
Slang terms your grandmother uses
Fear-based advertising
Con men
Middle school nerds stuffed in lockers
Ineffective over-the-counter pain relievers
Keyboards with one key that doesn't work
Expeditions to the North Pole in which
    everyone died

Value-added taxes
Yellow teeth
The loneliness of the long-distance runner
Bad fusion restaurants
Women who dye their eyebrows
Eating an entire gallon of ice cream
Babies who pull on your nose
Entry-level jobs
Overachievers
Underachievers
Mud-thick coffee
Celebrities with oversized heads
Companies that don't offer maternity leave
The Battle of Bull Run
Promiscuous nuns
Checking in with the office while on vacation
Apathy
Coming into work early and leaving late
Life coaches
German measles
The first year of medical school
Nostalgia for summer vacation
Getting the giggles at a funeral
Broken dams
Multitasking
Yeomen
Middle school girls who stuff their bras
Using reality TV shows to cast the leads in
    Broadway musicals
Useful fictions

Poisonous berries
Compulsory military service
Getting food poisoning on your wedding day
Drunken rednecks
Children who condescend to their parents
Being uninvited to a wedding
Rabid squirrels
Forgetting to think before speaking
Pathos
Bathos
Frozen carcasses
Toddlers who drink bleach
Finding out that there is no Tooth Fairy
The gruesome original endings of classic
    fairy tales
Indentured servants
Sex in socks
Teenage pregnancy
Being common as dirt
People who are gutted like fish
Plane crashes caused by moisture in sensors
Roll, pitch, and yaw
Being comforted in a language you don't
   understand
Murders in parking lots
Monsoons
Forgetting your crutches
Self-medication
Heat exhaustion
Representative Mark Foley

Ozymandias
The assassination of Benazir Bhutto
Bribery
Overly subtle innuendos
Insufficiently subtle innuendos
Teenage siblings forced to share a room
Mojave rattlesnakes
Making jokes other people don't understand
Ingratitude
Cruise missiles
Driving through raging blizzards
Having sex with your best friend's wife
Having sex with your best friend's husband
Stepping on broken glass with bare feet
Firewalking and getting burned
People who claim never to fight with their
    significant other
Copperhead snakes
Whiskey as a remedy for childhood illnesses
Voodoo
Chefs with tongue cancer
Accidentally eating pieces of eggshell
Beachcombing paupers
Gastric bypass surgery
The pathetic fallacy
Phone calls at 3 A.M.
Un–fair trade coffee
Ratty doormats
Novelizations
The winter of our discontent

Being scalded with hot oil
Public circumcisions
The West Memphis Three
Fashion shoots where models are dressed like
    homeless people
Death threats
Satanic rituals
Fucking the police
Getting lost in the woods
Drainage ditches
Hog-tying
Sweat behind the knees
Ugly minds
The decline of free range grazing
Waking up screaming
Being mounted by a stallion
Rusted tin roofs
Shotgun shacks
Impotence
The thirteenth fairy
Doing your laundry at a laundromat
Cockeyed optimists
People who are unable to afford lifesaving
    medical treatments
Damaged connective tissue
Relatives who don't come back from war
Thrill kills
Pencil stabbings
Sticky thighs
Mistaking vinegar for fruit juice

Bloating

Vacations that fail to rejuvenate you

Special education

Unreliable eyewitnesses

Getting friend requests from bands you have never heard of on MySpace

Glaring grammatical errors in your résumé

Parents who insist that their average children are gifted

People without teeth smiling

People who do bird calls

Sorting mail for eight hours a day

Not having an alibi

The American Express black card

Spending money you don't have

Bad sex that results in diseases

Good sex that results in diseases

Permanent injuries

Miscarriages

The waning of desire

Coercion

Slander

Pets with better health insurance than many people

Prison rape

Presidents who appoint their friends

Being followed by photographers

Not being followed by photographers

Gory details

Scratchy toilet paper

Twitching noses
Farting cats
Police ineptitude
Quick-rooting weeds
People thinking you're older than you
    actually are
Watching a cow die
Ear candling
The occult
Cotton Mather
Getting hit by a truck
Fried crickets
Getting stuck to the toilet seat
Lethal force
Endless winters
Babies with fangs
Cars that don't signal when they're turning
Heart attacks at weddings
Generational decreases in short-term memory
Ice cream cones the size of your head
Men who unbutton their shirts for the sole
    purpose of displaying chest hair
Ants in your pants
Ants in your kitchen
Lucky bastards
Sex scandals
Hummers driven by nineteen-year-old
    freshmen at state universities
Obstruction of justice
Plans for world domination

Adult diapers

Hardening of the arteries
International disputes over the origins of
    the potato
The decrease in average height following the
    agricultural revolution
Piles of viscera
Bludgeoning
Untimely death
Timely death
Plagues of locusts
Rocky mountain oysters
Arthropods
Rampant nationalism
Human sacrifice
Court-appointed lawyers
Bleeding hearts (metaphorical)
Bleeding hearts (literal)
The Battle of Bunker Hill
Being late for a job interview
Small kitchen fires
Tripe
Tongue
Prohibition
14,000 Things to Be Happy About by Barbara
    Ann Kipfer
Leaning too far out the window
Being blown up on your wedding day
Leotards
Thought police
Teenagers who don't get asked to prom

Indecipherable voice mails
Dueling as a means of settling disputes
Vikings
Humpty Dumpty
Dental dams
Rebel yells
Waiting for five hours to be on TV for five
    seconds
Waiting for Godot
Being forced to drink bacon grease
Sudden Infant Death Syndrome
Having a chair broken over your head
Drug interactions
Social interactions
Endless previews
The erosion of the Sphinx
Droit de seigneur
Nuns killed for what they believe
The Four Horsemen of the Apocalypse
Old westerns in which the bad guys are
    always Mexican
Cormac McCarthy novels in which the bad
    guys are always Mexican
Beating a dead horse
Beating a live horse
Laudanum
Grout
Clubs based on hatred of specific ethnic groups
Opium dens
Women who have a thing for murderers

The dregs of humanity
Colleges where you can major in enlightenment
Decent people suffering
Coughing blood
The O.K. Corral
Howitzers
Sprayed brain matter
Being told that everything will be okay
Sabotage between beauty pageant contestants
Erotic toe licking
Fingernails ripped off with pliers
Desperate older women
Being unable to distinguish between dirt and
    birthmarks
Having no one to meet your flight at the airport
Being exiled to the couch
Listing your height and weight on your
    résumé
Men who will accept only female roommates
Popular footage of fatal accidents
Phone sex at a pay phone
Finding your book in the half-off bin
Children who never come back from study
    abroad
Disappointing last lectures
Having your hair cut off as a prank
Being too weak to lift your battle axe
Taking a year to finish a book
Literalists
Racist cops who shoot black people

Wedding gowns of future divorcees
Lending to someone who dies
Rustlings in the undergrowth
Rushed sex
Scimitars dripping with blood
Children who know what sex is
Love poems recited in German
Radhakant Bajpai, who made the Guinness
    Book of World Records for having five
    inches of hair growing out of his ears
Failed open marriages
Failed closed marriages
Finding out you have cancer during a routine
    physical
Animosity between the Tutsis and the Hutus
    in Rwanda
Non-ironic wearing of capes
People who begin every sentence with "I may
    be wrong but"
The fading of initial excitement
Eating out with vegan friends
Underpaid public servants
Art as a negation of life
Seasonal alcoholism
Learning intimate facts about coworkers
Polydactyly—having extra fingers and toes
Mazes of government corridors
Solutions that create more problems
Reflexive disdain for the popular
People who read poetry literally

Being forced to perform mental arithmetic to
    a metronome
Traveling second class and getting pubic lice
Traveling first class and getting pubic lice
Riding bareback on a porcupine
People with multiple last names
Sickeningly wholesome children's books
The effect of habit on willpower
Water on cereal
Leisure ruined by anxiety about work
The smell of rotten eggs
Insects trapped in moving cars
Kamikaze moths
The impossibility of returning to the past
Fashionable mixtures of high- and lowbrow
    references
Teachers who compel student participation
Sentences that can't decide on a tense
Unheeded cries for help
Drunks operating chainsaws
Being trapped in a car that is slowly filling
    with water
Two people trying to share one pillow
Being unable to make someone angry
Only caring about people who look like you
Sex-related injuries
Losing your wedding band
Duck-and-cover drills
Pleasures tainted by association
Butter as hair gel

Being unsure whether something is a country
or a company
Transcripts from black box flight recorders
recovered from airplane crashes
Burning down your friend's house
People who stare at the TV while you talk
to them
Flavorless food
Feigned seizures
Sulfurous fumes seeping from sewers
Organic toilet paper
Ugly people trying to be sexy
The futility of resistance
Ineffective grassroots movements
Disowning your former self
Smoke stains from old fires
Being unable to get up
Overuse of the word "genius"
Exiled luminaries
Mistaking shadows for predatory beasts
Mistaking predatory beasts for shadows
Gore-stained graves of warriors
Hearing your neighbor beat his wife
Knowing your younger sibling had sex on
your bed
Being tired but unable to fall asleep
The ban on gays in the military
The glow of enemy campfires
Needing more than you're needed
Used condoms in meadows

Going to bed and never waking up
Disaster spectators
Old women throwing flower pots from
    high windows
Catered fast food
People who see puppies as life-affirming
Scooter-scooter collisions
Scooter–semi truck collisions
Drug mules
The defeat of Spartacus
The law of eminent domain
Selling open space to developers
T-shirts as art
The smell of industrial brass cleaner
Trying to distinguish between smog and clouds
Girlfriends referred to as "the latest"
Love-bruised hearts
Love-bruised faces
Hearing yourself on tape
Seeing yourself on tape
Nerve gas
Hating your job but loving the money
Privation in the midst of abundance
Staring at a computer screen when your
    eyes hurt
Accidentally sending intimate e-mails to the
    wrong person
Podiatry
The extermination of stray cats
Brains clogged with trivial facts

The confusion of price and value
Forced marches over rugged terrain
The survival rate of plane crashes
Suffocating etiquette
Projects converted to luxury high-rises
Moldy shower curtains
Being housebound
Opinions surrounded by caveats
Backyards next to highways
Yearning for the unattainable
Good deeds with bad motives
Bad deeds with good motives
Piercings done with paper clips
Vanity that grows with age
Concession speeches
The Happy Land social club fire
People who embrace themselves
Suicidal janitors
Middle seats
Apologies to "the public"
Trying and failing
Not really trying and succeeding
Not realizing your last words are your last words
Kids who pet dogs and get mauled
Organic farms turned into industrial factories
The guilt of the undeserving
Poor people who join the army
Petit mal seizures
Grand mal seizures
Feigned heart attacks

Opponents of interracial adoption
Graphing your bowel movements
Books you can't finish
Being trounced by a five-year-old at a
    board game
Avalanches
Killing the last member of a species
Halliburton
Fishing downstream from the local nuclear plant
Competitive suffering
Fearing bad news
Someone dying on your birthday
Watching other women hit on your husband
Dead messengers
Not getting the joke
Overworked sherpas
Using leftovers from funerals for weddings
Shrinking vocabulary size
Encephalized apes in suits
Graves' disease
Urinal conversationalists
Little boys who will one days be rapists
Spell-chanting hags
Headaches before your period
The phrase "Shut up, stupid"
Being waitlisted for college
Being waitlisted for heaven
Love Story
The belief that all problems are uniquely
    modern

Male ballerinas

Getting caught picking your nose

Lahars—huge waves of flowing mud triggered by volcanoes

Breaking someone else's dishes over their head

The last match when you're camping

Leaving all of your passwords on a public computer

Being visibly overjoyed to see someone who is indifferent to you

Being indifferent to see someone who is visibly overjoyed to see you

Chores before sunrise

Chores after sunrise

Kim Goodman, who is in the Guinness Book of World Records for popping her eyes half an inch out of their sockets

Worldviews inspired by the *Star Wars* movies

Running out of oxygen at the top of Mount Everest

Plants that never feel sunlight

People who never feel sunlight

Ten-year-olds who can speak at length about their parents' marital problems

Foreskin origami

Self-dissection (psychological)

Self-dissection (physical)

Facial rashes

Negative self-talk

Slaves crushed by falling rubble during the
    construction of the pyramids
Internet autodidacts
Compliments that involve comparing someone
    to Oprah
Glaring grammatical errors in the *New York
    Times*
My Little Ponies
Unpaid vacation
Choosing sleep over exercise
Choosing exercise over sleep
Secondary infections
Sex columnists
Mistaking hallucination for divine revelation
Dead people accidentally used as fertilizer
Dead people intentionally used as fertilizer
People who use "lunch" as a verb
The inevitable conflict between sustainable
    farming and the logic of industrial capitalism
Milton's blindness
People who forget that you are in the room
Self-massage that leads to injury
Fat people sitting on you
Quandaries
Being tipped over while using a Port-a-Potty
Disbarred lawyers
Suggested donations
Indiscreet cheating on final exams
Discreet cheating on final exams
Being asked the question "Which wife?"

The Puke Ray, which fires a burst of energy at
   a nausea-inducing frequency
Subtle nationalism in children's literature
Adults with doll collections
Gun shows where children can buy firearms
Flossing with a paper clip
People who borrow pens, chew on them, then
   give them back
Ads that urge you to buy expensive gifts for
   minor holidays
Jeff Gordon
Performance-enhancing drugs
Inheritance tax
Chafing
Black eyes
Gordon Ramsay
Ingrown toenails
Toxins found in farm-raised salmon
Sacrilege
Leprosy
Losing your place in a book
Musicals based on Disney movies
The wrong people wearing spandex
Proselytizing
Cum stains
Multiple sclerosis
People who don't know they smell
Halitosis
The Pennsylvania Turnpike
Monuments caked in bird shit

Afghan poppy fields

Drive-thru speakers

New studies indicating that one in four New
Yorkers has herpes

The eruptions of Mount Etna

Glaucoma

Dr. Jesse Lazear, who proved that mosquitoes
carry yellow fever by allowing himself to
be bitten by a mosquito that had bitten an
infected patient. He then died.

Dishonest mechanics

Zoo animals

Lab rats

The smiley face killers

Slow-motion fight sequences

Shantytowns

Gated communities

Social upheaval

Bad spin-offs of good TV shows

Carson Daly

Nearsightedness

Farsightedness

People who pay money to defecate on others

Missed deadlines

Sardines

Fungicide residues in fish

Muscle atrophy

Heat waves

Biohazards

Bottom feeders

Rural poverty
The stereotype of high-achieving, nerdy
    Asian-American students
People who talk down to children
Sycophants
Empty parodies
Foot binding in China
Cirrhosis of the liver
Happy families that are all alike
Unhappy families that are unhappy in their
    own ways
Mysterious disappearances
Henpecked husbands
The six kindergarteners hospitalized in New
    York after a boy found heroin and took it
    to his day care center
The death of Norman Mailer
Teachers' salaries
Curveballs
Petty theft
The underworld
Huntington's disease
Spreadsheets
Self-absorption
Free giveaways that you don't actually want
Baseballs thrown through windows
Child pornography
The pace of change
Wiretapping
Al-Qaeda

Stopgap solutions
Nancy Grace
Drug overdoses
Crohn's disease
The Days Inn just outside the Lincoln Tunnel
Accidents involving dynamite
Families murdered in their beds
Pants with stains at the crotch
"Springboards" that don't actually take you
    anywhere
The disappearance of the three-martini lunch
Roadblocks
Borderline Personality Disorder
Beached whales
People who look like beached whales
David Kaczynski, who was the first to discover
    that the Unabomber was his brother
Watching the Home Shopping Network for fun
Apathetic doctors
Losing your boarding pass
Broken furniture that is still being used
Trying to carry too many bags
Having to pay for bad food on airplanes
Overstaying your welcome
Traveling with small children
Awkward hugs
Internal bleeding
Having to buy generic brands
People who die mid-flight on airplanes
Not knowing what to do

Family therapy

Ten-year-olds on Prozac

Your ego

Not living up to your in-laws' expectations

Simon de Montfort, the English earl who
    induced cerebral hemorrhage by tickling
    captives' feet with a feather until they died
    of laughter

Polyester bed sheets

People who decide they don't want to die
    after they've leapt from a tall building, but
    before they hit the ground

People who wear more than one plaid

Nervous breakdowns at supermarkets

Fatal falls

Young children witnessing death for the first
    time

School janitors with pedophiliac tendencies

Obligatory sympathy

Forgetting your child's birthday

Your parents forgetting your birthday

The plight of Madame Bovary

Having to move out of your dream house

Public discussions about sexual dysfunction

Thin walls

Loud beds

Dyslexia

Public restrooms

Lectures from strangers

Lectures from friends

Overestimating your own brilliance
Forgotten children wandering the aisles of
grocery stores
The nuclear disaster at Three Mile Island
Leaving your ATM card in the ATM
Movies that romanticize orphans
Having extremely narrow feet
Never being able to find your size
Having nothing to say to your spouse
Shame in high school locker rooms
Being mistaken for your child's grandmother
The likelihood that your husband will die
before you do
The likelihood that your wife will outlive you
Copays
Cell phone bills
Half-broken toenails
Watery pasta sauce
Not having enough napkins
Getting caught stealing porn
Coming home from a tropical vacation to a
rainstorm
Expired credit cards
Insults prefaced by "No offense, but"
Train collisions
Accidentally being touched somewhere
inappropriate
Being touched somewhere inappropriate on
purpose
Clothes that don't fit you anymore

Beggars with cell phones
Delirium tremens, colloquially known as the
    trembling madness
The link between synthetic food colorings and
    restlessness and irritability in children
Your boyfriend's ex-girlfriend
Your girlfriend's ex-boyfriend
Littering
Being arrested for littering
People who live in train stations
New York City in August
People who go to yoga classes without
    wearing underwear
Paying a lot to attend the wedding of someone
    you don't really like
Dinner parties where all the food is bad
Small talk at funerals
Walking in on someone in the bathroom
Band-Aids that don't stick
Watching someone eat a Big Mac
Eating a Big Mac
The compulsive need to photograph yourself
Young professionals
Expensive shoes that hurt your feet
Musicals about the Holocaust
Moving out
Trying to motivate someone
Calling in sick to work and then running into
    your boss that night at a bar
Using the wrong preposition

Trying to get the ketchup out of the bottle
Tripping and falling in a public place
Waiters with unwashed hands
Taking a "break" from a relationship
Overpriced greasy diners
Getting a smaller tax rebate than you expected
People who write "sexual favors" in the memo
    line when they write you a check
Hair salons with puns in their names like
    "Shear Pleasure" and "A Cut Above"
Pipe bombs
Broken levees
The fact that the nation's suicide rate remains
    the same as it was in 1965
Practice that doesn't make perfect
Pimps
Agoraphobia
Body Dysmorphic Disorder
Malingerers
Pap smears
People with no impulse control
Hitting a brick wall
The problem of evil
Popsicles that melt all over your fingers
Spilling your drink on your date
Having free will and not exercising it
Gum disease
Celebrities who claim to be fixing a deviated
    septum when they are really getting a
    nose job

Peptic ulcers

Neon-colored food products

Conjoined twins

Earning more money than the man you're
  involved with

Earning less money than the woman you're
  involved with

Post-baby bodies

Celebrities whose post-baby bodies are
  exactly the same as their pre-baby bodies

Port-a-Potties

Introducing your children to people you're
  dating

"Subversives" beaten with rifle butts

Pretending to be talking on your cell phone
  when there's no one on the other line

Lactose intolerance

Freak accidents resulting in nails being driven
  into skulls

The link between erectile dysfunction and
  coronary heart disease

Fake orgasms

Hating your family

Hating your feet

Andropause—the waning of testosterone that
  occurs as men age

The death of Heath Ledger

The fact that the average chain restaurant
  entrée contains 867 calories

Prunes

Prudes

Uterine fibroids

People who attempt suicide by drinking rubbing alcohol

Job interviews

"Earring Magic Ken"—an early '90s Ken doll with a pierced ear and a purple mesh T-shirt

Insurgents

The burning of Joan of Arc

The canonization of Joan of Arc

Diverticulitis

Shin splints

Student drivers

Student pilots

The dying of the light

The Black Prince

Alleys in Cairo at dusk

Attempts at levity in corporate settings

Knitwear

Homeless men who mutter in the corners of cafeterias

Tactful attempts to ascertain your mental stability

Emotionally distant fathers

Smothering mothers

Drunken vows of undying love

Drunken conceptions of children

The relentlessness of advertising

People who have favorite TV commercials

Mechanical metaphors for sex (like drill, hammer, pound, etc.)

The number of people that could be fed if
    movie star salaries were cut in half
The deaths of dogs
Dentists with Parkinson's disease
Bleeding gums
Urinary tract infections
The screeching noise of subway brakes
Food particles in facial hair
Light pollution
Distant train whistles
The fact that there are more McDonald's in
    the world than hospitals
The "final solution"
Veneers of erudition
The justification of suffering as a necessity for
    creating great art
Childhood idols who commit suicide with
    shotguns
Fashionable pseudosciences
Oblique boasting
People who eat well, exercise, don't smoke,
    and still die young
Pretending to understand abstract art
People who cough during concerts
People who think they're wiser because
    they're older
Failed attempts to domesticate squirrels
Mysterious diseases that baffle doctors and
    then kill you
Elevator small talk

Orpheus

Eurydice

The number of books an average American
reads each year

Overspecialization

The fate of Barry Lyndon

Solitary meals

Being kicked in the ass

Compulsively Googling yourself

Trying to hang yourself from a tree branch
that can't support your weight

Oedipus complexes

The thieves crucified next to Christ

The extinction of gentleman scholars

Thalidomide babies

High-fructose corn syrup

The triumph of death

The shooting of horses

The smell of putrid meat

Rich people

Poor people

Diversionary foreign wars

The forty-hour work week

The eighty-hour work week

The unknowable

Marijuana-induced metaphysical conversations

Sunday evenings

The shortest day of the year

Headfirst dives into shallow swimming pools

Corrupt tour guides

Medea's children
Mid-afternoon despair
Tantalus
Idealization of the French
People who sing out loud to their iPods
Misuse of the word "existentialism"
The Third Reich
Invented words that end in "tron"
Killer bees
Ostentatious philanthropists
Diesel fuel
Catching your kids having sex
Catching your kids having sex with your spouse
Nitpicky classical music critics
Parents who crush their children's self-esteem
The sound of gargling
Loud people in enclosed spaces
Poorly made condoms
Harelips
Exes who want to get back together with you
People who grunt during spinning class
People who don't wipe down machines at the
    gym after using them
Unhealthy weight loss induced by the desire
    to look perfect on your wedding day
Trichotillomania—a disorder characterized by
    the urge to rip out your hair
The Revolutionary War
Cosmetic procedures performed by untrained
    physician's assistants

Tan-orexics
People on ventilators
Triple bypass surgery
Stuntmen who are killed on film sets
The establishment
CDs that skip
Murders without motive
Hysterectomies
Exploratory surgery
Blindness
Sudden cardiac death
School shootings
Angioplasty
People who insist on having the last word
Malfunctioning fire alarms
The Franco-Prussian War
Husbands who publicly chide their wives
People who mistake flattery for praise
Love killed by ambition
Prohibited topics of conversation
Being chastised for trivial errors
Married men who hire only pretty secretaries
Married men who hire only pretty secretaries
    and then have sex with them
Terrible books translated into thirty-seven
    languages
Men who are always asking their wives to be
    more like their mothers
People who deny the legitimacy of all motives
    but their own

Scraping by to keep up appearances

Careers spoiled by marriages

Marriages spoiled by careers

Coming home from college to find you no longer have a bedroom

Coming home from college to find your parents are no longer married

Genius without character

Finding the lover who promised to wait up for you sound asleep

Chronically abusive husbands who swear this was the last time

People who speak softly and carry a big stick

People who speak loudly and carry a small stick

People who don't speak at all and carry a submachine gun

Smart children teased until they conceal their intelligence

"Staycations"—vacations spent at home

Candles burned at both ends

Husbands who refuse to use a hair brush

Men whose sense of style consists of two states: wearing clothes and not wearing clothes

Having to praise bad cooking

Kissing someone who has just eaten gorgonzola cheese

Speaking poorly of your wife to your kids

Discussing the digestion process during a meal

Being told "ask your mother"

Being told "ask your father"

People whose presence causes laughter to stop

The fact that corpses feel heavier than live bodies

People who claim to see the face of Jesus in inanimate objects

Aaron Burr

Overpopulation

The massacre of the Huguenots

Celebrities who make millions of dollars before they turn eighteen

The possibility that your cell phone will catch fire when you pump gas

People who are self-righteous about practicing yoga

Ill-advised flings

Porn addiction

Getting caught by your kids having sex

Getting caught by your parents having sex

Cruelty to circus animals

Dirty feet

Splenda

Onychomycosis—a fungal infection of the toenail

Shortness of breath

Solitary confinement

Getting the placebo in a double-blind study

People who pick their noses in public

Tearing a hole in your favorite jeans

Trying to find matching socks in the morning

Pouffy prom dresses

Corporations
People who talk about marriage on the first date
Misappropriation of hedge funds
Children on reality TV shows
Four-inch heels
Dander
Dead skin flakes
The uselessness of the appendix
Love children
Meaningless points of etiquette
Food prices at airports
Dying alone in a nursing home
Embezzlement
People who can't make up their minds about
    whether they want to date you
Lifting with your back instead of your knees
Manicurists who can't afford manicures
Bad productions of good plays
Foreign janitors who were college professors
    in their native countries
Drunken tourists
The Soviet Union
Being in a pressure cooker (metaphorically)
Being in a pressure cooker (literally)
Bedpans
Choking on throat lozenges
Osteoporosis
Conversations that start with: "If you could go
    back in time and kill Hitler . . ."
Forensic pathologists

Taxidermy
Seeing your face in a magnifying mirror
Seeing your ass in a magnifying mirror
Being pressured to get married
Archaic institutions
Fertilizer runoff
Gasoline additives in tap water
Forgetting to pack socks when you go on
    vacation
Teenagers who cut themselves
Blackmail
Being the new kid at school
Torrential downpours
Bad harvests
Uranium
The Vietcong
Gender wars
"Green noise"—an overload of contradictory
    messages on how to save the environment
Struggling nonprofits
Playing tennis with someone who cheats
Apple martinis
Cranky train conductors
Running out of battery power on your
    cell phone
Robert Wadlow, the world's tallest man, who was
    8 feet 11 inches and died at age twenty-two
Missed layups
Crusty eyes
Overbooked flights

Finding out that your boyfriend is into pain-related porn

Disappointing magazine articles about interesting people

Bad film critics

Putting the family dog to sleep

Morning sickness

Discovering that your Neosporin is expired after you've cut yourself

Realizing too late that your husband shouldn't be doing your taxes himself

Backpacks that don't last as long as you think they should

Shoes with toes poking through them

DVDs that freeze

Bad kissers

Hate crimes

Fake relics of saints

People who borrow money and don't pay it back

Men who growl as an attempt to initiate sex

Chipping your nails right after you've had them done

Electric razors that break when you're halfway done shaving

Dogs that lick you after drinking out of the toilet

Not being carded

The fact that your mother knows you masturbate

Miners who died underground during the California Gold Rush

Mixed messages

Thirteen-year-olds who constantly wear
    Harvard T-shirts
E-mail solicitations from online universities
Revision
Being unable to remove your date's bra
Being unable to remove your date's pants
Rivers near chemical plants
Rogue nuclear rings
Roger Clemens
Fringed moccasins
Threnodies
Overhearing snippets of intimate
    conversations in public
The worship of status
The arbitrariness of fashion
Teenage girls who glorify anorexia
De facto segregation
De jure segregation
The scarcity of meaningful work
Couples who walk with their hands in each
    other's back pockets
Ethical compromises
Popes murdered by poison
Abortions performed with coat hangers
Death by bludgeoning
Realizing that your parents must have
    conceived you somehow
Motherly paranoia
Walking stereotypes
People who emulate characters on TV shows

The twenty-fourth mile of the marathon
Marsh flies
The perils of flattery
The illusion of democracy
Persistent vegetative states
Neglected, moss-covered graves
The realization that death is permanent
Accidental racism
Attempts at manliness
Fake emergencies
Real emergencies
Journalism
Generic suburban families
Dramatically gored matadors
Displaced rage
Bizarrely competitive amateur athletes
Old women in fishnets
Trying to take ridiculous people seriously
Being paid to take ridiculous people seriously
Morbid self-reflection
The plot of porn films
Death row inmates who are later exonerated
Camping trips on which somebody gets eaten
    by a bear
People who hate the things you love
People who hate the people you love
Romantic depictions of war
Predictable plots
Kindergartners with hours of homework
Obsequious pedants

Fathers who didn't actually want kids
The grandchildren of Nazis
Plucking your eyebrows
Not plucking your eyebrows
Novels forgotten on trains
Contested wills
Corporate law firms
Unintentional rudeness
Intentional rudeness
Village idiots
The distant howling of wolves
Incompetent surgeons
The Jim Crow laws
Swarming cockroaches
The hegemony of science
Microwaving food in plastic containers
Fashionably pre-frayed jeans
Irrational fears of common household objects
Leeches
Uncontrollable violent thoughts
Needlessly detailed naturalistic novels
Chronic pain
Mephitic vapors
Farm distress after the Civil War
Being forced to watch home videos of your
     significant other's childhood
Beautiful dreams you can't remember after
     you wake up
Purposelessness
Vanishing oral cultures

Senior citizens who want to die
Senior citizens who don't want to die
Days when it's too hot to touch other people
Bloated imperial empires
Woeful ignorance of history
Losing feeling in your extremities
Manipulative use of statistics
Unsafe drinking water
Dust-covered family heirlooms
The law of primogeniture
The sinking of the *Lusitania*
Menial workers who are forced to wear name
    tags and smile
Race car drivers who die in fiery crashes
Having a black cat cross your path
Being crucified and forsaken
Hidden campaign contributions
Eating on the subway
Being heckled on the streets of foreign countries
Anterior ischemic optic neuropathy
Hidden hotel charges
Viruses that make your computer visit kiddie
    porn sites
Sandbags
Scathing judgments of others that just make
    you feel worse
Pockmarks
Credit card companies that make their
    customers look like worse credit risks
    than they actually are

Fruitcake

Late fees

People who do magic tricks at bars

Entrepreneurs whose livelihood depends on the gullibility of the public

Trying to correct errors with White-Out

Vioxx—an anti-inflammatory drug that MAY have caused as many as 139,000 heart attacks

Derelicts

Bronchitis

Getting an infection due to poor hospital sanitation

The price of drinks from hotel minibars

Heart murmurs

Living hundreds of miles from the nearest person you might want to have sex with

Mysterious shadows on mammograms

Selling out

The Israeli athletes murdered during the Munich Olympics

The Haymarket Affair—a violent riot in 1886

Children who play with guns

Statutory rape

Drinking too much and embarrassing yourself in front of your coworkers

New York City trash that ends up in New Jersey landfills

Don Imus calling the Rutgers women's basketball team "nappy-headed hos"

Calling out the wrong name during sex
People who leave the air conditioning on
    when they're not home
Forgetting to throw out the food in the fridge
    before you go on a long vacation
Walking in heels on cobblestone streets
Abandoned mine shafts
Women with squeaky voices
Black holes
The songs that play on music boxes
Being tailgated
Wearing sackcloth
Egg timers
Peritonitis
Snow blindness
The abyss
Plastic utensils
Throwaway money
The San Francisco quake and fire of 1906
Neon signs with missing letters
Cinderblock
Petrified cat shit
St. Jude, patron saint of lost causes
Epilepsy
Bad slasher movies
Violent anarchists
People who chew on ice
Lou Gehrig's disease
Falling asleep in a chair
Discount butchers

Melting asphalt

Sauerkraut

Weight gain caused by birth control pills

Nervous tics

Cigarette burns

Raskolnikov

Thorazine

Having sex in a room with a door that
doesn't lock

Dan Quayle

Just saying no to drugs

Just saying yes to drugs

Urine stains

Pogroms

Christmas tree lights where one dead bulb
makes the whole strand stop working

Being too young to drive

Being too old to drive

Faulty wiring

Breaking the heel on your shoe

Euthanasia

Severed feet washed up on shore

Dogs accidentally sucked up and killed by
street sweepers

Quitting smoking, only to take it up again in
times of stress

Giving birth

Car payments

Empty nest syndrome

Straitjackets

Obituary typos

The smell of fertilizer

Explaining death to a small child

Men who can't tie their ties

Broken flip-flops

Vulgarity

Chloroform

Being in a hotel room next door to a crying infant

"Radio edits" of songs with all the curse words deleted

The curse of the goat

One-hit wonders

The American addiction to McDonald's

The accuracy of Wikipedia

Electrical outlets that don't work

Short fuses

Race riots

Being lost at sea

Ties for Father's Day

Hallmark cards

Digging a grave in dry, rocky soil

Kids who don't wear bike helmets

Accidentally discovering naked photos of yourself on the internet

Accidentally discovering naked photos of your significant other on the internet

Laika, the brave Soviet dog launched into space in 1957. She did not survive.

Professional wrestling

Surveillance
Police states
People who are born with a silver spoon in
    their mouth
Crack houses
Walking under a ladder
The cracked hands of cleaning workers
Friday the 13th
The Exxon Valdez oil spill
Incurring punitive damages
Dilapidated playgrounds
Video game addictions
Roommates who sing in the shower
Monotonous daily routines
Trust fund babies
Companies with high worker turnover
The vacant stares of passersby
Tyrants
Phrenology
People who can't match their clothes
Paralyzing self-consciousness
Testicular cancer
Undetectable yet deadly gas leaks
Incurable diseases
Frostbitten toes
Yellow journalism
Transience
Transients
Crevasses
Incessant urban noise

Garbage strikes
Happy people in advertisements
Dopamine depletion
Jocasta
Waving back at someone who wasn't actually
    waving at you
Being hit in the face by an apple core tossed
    from a car
Inadvertent grimaces
Tourists gazing at ruins
Sleep apnea
Sickeningly sweet cocktails
The mundane
Sad gorillas in zoos
Fragile ecosystems
Beautiful stupid people
Love at first sight
Feigned interest
Unaffectionate parents
Elderly people falling on the sidewalk
Bears that rummage in trash cans and
    frighten neighborhood children and then
    have to be killed
The difficulty of breaking bad habits
Intemperate wrath
People who weren't held enough as babies
Possessive lovers
Anticlimactic reunions
Defining yourself through your taste in TV
    shows

Small acts of rudeness
Revenge killings
Not being in college anymore
False prophets
Corporate metaphors (on board, in the loop, etc.)
Back-stabbing (metaphorical)
Back-stabbing (literal)
The idea that suffering makes you stronger
Food service workers called "sandwich artists"
Janitors called "particle alignment engineers"
Foreplay with motor oil
People who talk about things they know
    nothing about
Uxoriousness
Dying a virgin
Having to stop and talk to casual
    acquaintances at the grocery store
Muggings in Mexico City
Bad listeners
Botched circumcisions
Trash-strewn highway medians
Wars of succession
Wars of secession
Neglecting to patent an idea that would have
    made you millions
Washed-up former athletes
Recent studies showing that the average
    American's body contains 148 different
    synthetic chemicals
Starving to death in the Alaskan bush

Self-taught dentists
Dying in public
Vast menacing bureaucracies
Billionaires
Altitude sickness
People who lack a sense of wonder
The comparatively small percentage that the
    U.S. spends on foreign aid
Pinched radial nerves
Vestibulary disorders
Getting alcohol poisoning on a first date
Ketchup without any lycopene
Haplessness
Osteonecrosis of the jaw
Corporate dress codes
Fallen aristocrats
Politically correct euphemisms
Being taken for granted
Scams that trick elderly people out of their life
    savings
People who are too eager to practice their
    Spanish
Spinster great aunts
People who believe their mothers' opinions of
    them
Small dogs that are eaten by wild animals
Sex in bar bathrooms
Hand dryers that don't really get your hands dry
People who wear cowboy hats to parties
Mountain lion attacks

Jokes that begin: "Old [insert plural noun]
    never die, they just . . ."
Hypothermia
Hyperthermia
Wind-whipped snow blowing into your face
Kids with walkie-talkies
Climbers who perish on Mount Everest
Manipulation
Severe weather
Cold, clammy hands
Men who name their penises
Pickled body parts
Zombies
Date rape
Hypoxic dementia
Military police
Pelvic exams
Incoherent drunkenness
Subzero wind chill
People without opposable thumbs
Dog drool
Being punched in the nose
The reptilian brain
Rictuses of agony
Endocrine disruptors—chemicals that
    interfere with the hormones in our bodies
Being told you look tired
Being stopped by the police on a first date
Not honoring your father and your mother
Wage slaves

Not answering your phone, only to find that the
	person who's calling is standing across the
	street watching you not answer your phone
Penury
People who write bad science fiction as a hobby
Felonies
Kidneys as food product
Row houses
Pre-employment drug testing
Going down in flames
Tracheotomy holes
Congeners—impurities in alcohol that lead to
	more severe hangovers
Managers
Ketchup stains on tables
People who complain that immigrants are
	taking over the country
Flophouses
Offal
Sinks clogged with scraps of lettuce
Restrooms without any soap
Hypoglycemia
Back spasms
The fact that before 1998, workers had no
	federally mandated right to bathroom breaks
Stalkers
The floors of dive bars
Mystery novels you figure out before they're
	over
Aching feet

Cherry trees after all of their blossoms have fallen
Lye
Endless possibilities
Polls that predict election results inaccurately
Popped collars
People who wear clothes once and then return them
Waiting for your dining companion to come back from the bathroom
Capri pants
L.A. traffic
Slate-gray skies
Public armpit scratching
Public crotch scratching
People who pretend to read *The New Yorker* to look sophisticated
The media
The massacre of Armenians by the Turkish government from 1895–1922
Elections with only one candidate on the ballot
Hearing mice scurrying in the walls
Polls showing that 18 percent of Americans think the sun revolves around the earth
Source amnesia
North Korea's nuclear weapons program
Rising HIV diagnosis rates among young gay men
Kristallnacht

Unnecessary surgery
Breath that smells like chili
Warmongers
Driving into a snowbank
London fog
Organic pollutants found in Arctic penguins
Artificial butter flavoring
Realizing you forgot one ingredient for your
    recipe and having to go back to the store
    to get it
King George III
Bored retirees
Accidentally stumbling into a wasps' nest
Cafes where you have to pay for wireless access
Garbage washed up on the beach
Rivers running red with blood
Giles Corey—a suspected witch crushed to
    death by stone weights in 1692
Child abuse
Candy from strangers
Abu Ghraib
Military contractors
Windstorms
The Downing Street Memo
The North American Man-Boy Love Association
Mausoleums
Grounded flights
Swimming pools crowded with screaming
    children
Acrophobia

Mitochondrial disorders
Mount Vesuvius
Poor motor skills
Islamic militants
Standing water
Teenage drivers
Jaundice
Perjury
Children decapitated by roller coaster
    malfunctions
Hiccups
Dolphins stranded in New Jersey rivers
The shrieking of air raid sirens
Lumbar punctures
Having your hair pulled
People who talk about their exes on the first
    date
The imprisonment of Nelson Mandela
Armed rebels in Nigeria
Violent thugs
Hydrocephalic babies
Burning oil towers
Stress-related illnesses
Parents who sacrifice everything to give their
    children the opportunities they never had
Child brides
Radiation exposure from CT scans
Exploitation
Dot matrix printers
Shortness of breath

Plaque on the teeth

Plaque in the brain

Winona Ryder in department stores

Excommunication

Broken glass on playgrounds

People who claim to enjoy challenges

People who find fame via YouTube videos of
themselves acting stupid

Screws that break when you're trying to
fasten something

Husbands who can't fix anything

Going through the mail of the person you
just had sex with to figure out their name
before they wake up

Compromises

"Meet cute" in chick flicks

Speech impediments

Planned phone dates to catch up with friends

Attending your significant other's office
Christmas party

Getting cat hair all over your shirt

Canceled flights

Blurred boundaries

Having a self-defeating attitude

Interventions

Adopted children who are teased that their
parents bought them

Tailspins

Fat camp

Realizing that your life has become a cliché

Anal fixations

Sublimating your cravings

Coping mechanisms

Poems you were forced to study in high
   school English classes

Baseball bats used in self defense

Your Achilles' heel

Papilledema—optic disc swelling associated
   with brain tumors

Barking terriers

Laziness

Whooping cough

Being too drunk to remember your wedding

Trying to lift a heavy suitcase into the
   overhead compartment and dropping it on
   someone's head

Croup

Donald Rumsfeld

Cavities

Arachnoid cysts

Fat arms

Meningitis

People who claim their lives are perfect

Being hung over at work

Drastically falling birthrates in European
   countries

People who bring lots of uninvited guests to
   parties

Tuesdays with Morrie by Mitch Albom

Pseudo-wisdom

Losing your religion
Suicide bombers
People who shoot up kindergartens
Zookeepers who lose limbs to large animals
Trying to drive a car without snow tires in a
    blizzard
Septic tanks
Hello Kitty
Men who refuse to grow up
The Central Park jogger
Kenny G
Falling in love with someone who is allergic to
    your pet
Soapboxes and the people on them
Clear Channel
Dependency on sleeping pills
Negative publicity
Others forgetting favors they owe you
Funeral flowers
Undercooked steak
Overcooked steak
People who pop their zits in public
Couples who groom each other like monkeys
National monuments that are smaller than you
    expected
Applebee's
Americanized ethnic food
Lighthearted teenagers at the Holocaust
    Museum
Yoko Ono

Football teams named after ethnic slurs about
 Native Americans
Leaving your credit card at a bar after a night
 of drinking
Small business failures
Concerts to save Africa
Concerts to save the planet
Having your head shoved in a toilet
The fact that only 20 percent of Americans
 recycle magazines, though magazine
 recycling is available in 70 percent of
 American communities
Sharecroppers
People who believe that God hates gay people
Heretics burned at the stake
Walter Reed Hospital
Canned green beans
Physical therapy
Foods that never taste as good as the versions
 your mother made of them
Land mines
Debridement
Nasal sprays that make you lose your sense
 of smell
Staph infections
Bacterial vaginosis
Triage
Karaoke night at the local bar
Shady surgeons who use discounted body
 parts in transplant operations

Torpedoes

Golden showers

Dwarfism

Dioxin

The egos of great chefs

People who think the Heimlich maneuver is a
sexual position

Baby lotion commercials that make it look like
new mothers are happy and well-rested

Nonrefillable hydrocodone prescriptions

Feeling guilty about not replacing all your
appliances with energy-efficient models

Trying to read *Finnegan's Wake*

Campaign smears

Smear campaigns

People who see themselves as the
embodiment of common sense

People who define themselves based on their
favorite beer

Concealed weapons

Canker sores

Coffee stains on ties

Smoky fogs in casinos

People who stay virgins until marriage

Losing a fist fight in front of your date

School districts that are cutting down on
busing to save fuel costs

The future of Social Security

Having important documents sent to the
wrong mailing address

The 1973 oil crisis

Biting flies

The Red Summer of 1919

Cruel and unusual punishment

Beverly Hills

The Golden Triangle of illicit opium
production in Southeast Asia

Mopping the floor

Running out of dish soap when you have dirty
dishes

Having nothing to lose

Misquoted song lyrics

Students held back a grade

Stigmatization

Trichomoniasis—an STD that causes burning
and itching

People who are forced to give away their pets
due to home foreclosures

Mindless eating

Regretting things you didn't do

Regretting things you did do

Trying a new sport . . . and being terrible at it

Getting sand in your eyes at the beach

Sleeping badly

Men who own only corduroy suit jackets

Not having anyone sign your high school
yearbook

Moldy bathmats

Bed rest

The Tower of Babel

Temperatures in the Libyan desert
Children raised by wolves
Gloating
Bad improv comedy
Downtown streets closed for road races
The human awareness of death
Cocktail wieners
Algebra
Having too many cooks
Sixty-five-year-olds with Farrah Fawcett haircuts
Napoleon on Elba
Sagging sofas
Hearing lobsters scream as you cook them
Anal leakage
Going to bed angry
Sports cars purchased to alleviate midlife crises
Prostitutes purchased to alleviate midlife crises
The Aflac duck
Migrating geese as a harbinger of winter
Killer whales
Being unable to make an omelet without
    breaking some eggs
Little girls who want to be ballerinas when
    they grow up
The lonely sound of foghorns
Prison food
Pasta salads that have been sitting out at a
    picnic for several hours
Letting the cat out of the bag
Abdominal pain

Fever
Bacteria in raw poultry
Swollen glands
Having your tonsils out
Confusion
Sinus infections
Flying on airplanes with sinus infections
The fact that cold viruses can survive for up
   to three hours on objects like telephones
   and railings
Spitting
PMS
Mudslides (the drink)
Mudslides (the natural disaster)
Commercials that promise miracle weight loss
Forgetfulness
Mood swings
Cankles
Sore losers
Sore winners
Endometriosis
Your genes
Pelvic Inflammatory Disease
Birth defects
Lesions
Burping
Studies that show that most parents are
   happier grocery shopping or sleeping than
   spending time with their kids
Tiny drops of blood in the brain

Criminals impersonating police officers

Jumping the shark

Kleptomania

Dogs that run away

Standing up for your principles despite the cost

The fact that crime often does pay

Innocents abroad

Kidney failure

Deafness

Amputations performed with whiskey as an
anesthetic

Ambivalence

Waking up feeling as if your tongue is coated
with fur

Jackets that look like small furry animals

Jean-Claude "Baby Doc" Duvalier

White go-go boots

T-shirts with palm trees on them

Toe socks

Socks with fringe

Adults who wear Mickey Mouse watches

Housewives who constantly wear workout
clothes and never work out

SUVs with Starfleet Academy bumper stickers

Men who always smell like garlic

Thirty-year-olds who own no shoes except flip
flops

Thirty-year-olds who own no shoes except
sneakers

Rhinestone bras

Women who wear Mrs. Claus dresses each
   Christmas
The concept of a five-minute face
Leopard print dresses at school board meetings
Lava
Lava lamps
People who wear only black
People who think they can buy ski clothes
   only in Aspen
Women who constantly wear huge amounts of
   turquoise jewelry
Mothers who borrow their daughters' clothing
Velvet Elvis paintings
Panic disorders
Women who never cut their hair
Men who never cut their hair
Cotton T-shirts that shrink after one washing
Constant change in women's fashion
No change year after year in men's fashion
Ties that light up
Old women who wear headbands
Families who write optimistic Christmas
   letters each year
Denim overalls
Bits of bloody meat falling from open mouths
Medical personnel who wear scrubs on the
   weekend
Nine-year-olds in heavy makeup at the mall
Leaving your favorite scarf behind at a
   restaurant

Stirrup pants
Escalator collapses
Waiting for someone who never arrives
Peeling an orange and getting your fingers
    sticky
Chocolate that tastes like wax
The Furies
Globalization
Exchanging money in foreign countries
Arriving late to a show
Drunk people urinating in fountains
Bad reggae music
The shaking of infants
Used cars
People who invent words in order to make
    song lyrics rhyme
Pickpockets
Farting in elevators
Children's books that contain sexual metaphors
Office supply shortages
People who cheat at board games
Getting snapped with a rubber band
Your naked body
Sulfuric acid
People who don't wash their hands after using
    the bathroom
Temperatures at the North Pole
Drinks served in soapy glasses
Unflushed toilets
Looking like your boyfriend's mother

Looking like your girlfriend's father
Sniffling
Licorice toothpaste
Thinking somebody likes you who actually
    doesn't
Men who are obsessed with threesomes
Burned bits of food on the bottom of the oven
Safe-crackers
Leftover fish
Comas
Bubble children
Gravity
Rains of frogs
Stories with morals
Nondairy creamer
Pregnancy scares
Trying to figure out the proper plurals of
    words derived from Latin
Needing crutches
Dogs that eat chocolate and die
Driving in the fog
Overly air-conditioned office buildings
Insufficiently air-conditioned office buildings
Plastic plants
The smell of unwashed hair
Celebrity baby names
Nightclub fires
Trash bags that break while you're taking out
    the garbage
Wanting to go back to bed

Prematurely
born puppies

People who advocate drilling in national parks
Trying to eat spaghetti with a spoon
Tanks
Losing investors
Seagulls stealing your ice cream at the beach
Worn boot heels
Microphone feedback
Rain at outdoor parties
Empty fire extinguishers
Used napkins
Busy signals
Martha Stewart
Embarrassing nicknames
Catwoman
Hotel room art
Being alone on holidays
Awkward exposition
Hair after rainstorms
Drowned rats
The graveyard shift
Cutting your finger while chopping vegetables
Women who dress like drag queens
Unidentified stains on motel mattresses
Bad photos of you
People who try to profit from disasters
Prejudice
Forgetting to feed your fish
Taking one step forward and two steps back
Spot treatments
Breakouts on your wedding day

Being asked: "You and what army?"

Infomercials

People with chiseled abs

Turning yourself orange while trying to use self-tanner

Dramatic elimination ceremonies on reality shows

People who know only one or two words in a foreign language but use them constantly

Wishing your hair looked like the hair in shampoo commercials

Chemotherapy

Being poorly astrologically matched with your significant other

Poison ivy

Cracked feet

Getting in an accident with a larger vehicle

Nasty surprises

Harpoons

Velour

Having to wash dishes to cover the cost of your meal

Thin people who eat all the time

Losing whole afternoons to marathons of bad TV shows

Wal-Mart

Babies spitting up on you

The higher incidence of snoring among the obese

Cyclists at night without reflector lights

Prominent ears
Prominent noses
Knobby elbows
Weak chins
The unlikelihood that you will ever be a
    rock star
Yard work
Dandelions
Watching your ex groping their new lover
Texas chainsaw massacres
Alarmists
Distress signals
Midair collisions of commercial airliners
The Boxer Rebellion
Tiananmen Square
Thorns
Putting metal products in the microwave
Putting paper products in the oven
Kissing a man who hasn't shaved
The teenagers on MTV's *My Super Sweet
    Sixteen*
Pets scared by fireworks
Vapidity
Irresponsible research
Toddlers wearing designer clothing
Towns where the biggest event is the weekly
    high school football game
Magic 8 Balls that are wrong
Losing money at billiards
Hustlers

Soft spots in your teeth

Muscular dystrophy

IRA bombings

Unidentified sources cited in gossip
magazines

Not knowing the name of your child's father

Foot dermatitis

Children working in factories

People who are shot as they reach for their
wallets by cops who think they're reaching
for guns

Being blindsided

Children who grow up on tour buses

Book groups that never talk about books

Being referred to as "fresh meat"

Shivs—makeshift knives, popular among
prison inmates

Sucking in your gut

Defenses

Getting caught skipping class

Incredibly expensive cancer drugs

Dubious benefits

Schistosomiasis—a parasitic disease caused
by snails

Hijackers

Nematodes

Infectious disease specialists who accidentally
infect themselves with diseases

Great runners who get cramps during
important races

Bear baiting
Gossip columnists
Realizing the person you're speaking to is
     wearing headphones
Realizing the person you're speaking to is deaf
Viral marketing campaigns that fail to
     generate any buzz
Children on milk cartons
Buckets with holes
Inadequate safety regulations
Poorhouses
Sex offenders that live in your neighborhood
Paying $100 for a tank of gas
Suicidal impulses
Circular logic
Heads stuck in ovens
Aridity
Trial separations
Benzaldehyde
The ease with which Americans can purchase
     guns
Countries without public education
Corruption in the Italian political system
Unpasteurized milk
Your personal hell
Broken dreams
Oppressed nonentities
Bank robbers
Bad severance packages
Cities under siege

Wishing your life was more like a Meg
  Ryan movie
Bullet-riddled Humvees
Inept homicide units
Having to wait a whole week to find out what
  happens next on your favorite TV show
Fatal flaws
The beating of Rodney King
Dysfunctional families
Makeovers you can't replicate at home
Irritable pregnant women on hot days
Cocktail prices at L.A. bars
Social obligations
Getting friend requests on Facebook from
  people you don't actually know
Being a third wheel
Sunday school
Psychiatric hospitalization
Melting ice floes
Getting a run in your stockings
Men who look up schoolgirls' skirts on the
  subway
Feeling obligated to buy crafts manufactured
  by your friends
Receiving jewelry that you would never
  actually wear
Having your proposal of marriage rejected
Code Blue
Anthrax
People who are more talented than you

People who constantly quote TV shows you've never seen

Running out of your medications before you have a chance to refill them

The cable going out

The air conditioning going out

The fact that the U.S. is one of only two countries where pharmaceuticals can be advertised on television

Great TV shows that get canceled

The fact that 20 percent of Americans don't pay their taxes

Knowing the best years of your life are already over

Overreacting

Uncertainty

Victorian chimneysweeps

Low-flying planes

Metabolic wastes

The Witness Protection Program

Compounds encircled by barbed wire

Hard labor

Crocodile attacks

Trying to find a needle in a haystack

Siberian prison camps

Children blinded by fireworks

Evil sorcerers

Missing someone

Shivering

Slime

Belly flops
Falling rocks
Tracking dogs
Roll call
Hailstorms
Digging in frozen ground
Firing squads
Boggy wastelands
The 1918 Spanish flu pandemic, which killed
    50 million people worldwide
Goblins
Fugitives from justice
The iron maiden
The band Iron Maiden
Disappointment
Dreams deferred
Poisoned wine
The squeaky wheel getting the grease
Tranquilizer darts
Being stabbed with a pitchfork
Stillborn babies
The Chinese laborers who died building
    American railroads
Having a sore throat
Chauffeurs who aren't allowed to speak to
    their passengers
Bared teeth
Shouts of alarm
Ambushes
Crash landings

The wailing of ambulances
Falling for your best friend's ex
Falling for your ex's best friend
Seeing your own entrails
Grunt work
The serpent in the Garden of Eden
Unmet quotas
Stalin
Shirkers
Pieces of flair
Mao's Great Leap Forward
Dickensian paupers
Distant gunshots
Bricks thrown through windows
Burst eardrums
Killing fields
Being called a coward
The squawking of chickens
The taste of blood
The radio dissolving into static just as your
    favorite song comes on
Forgetting to feed the pets you're pet-sitting
Forgetting to feed the children you're
    babysitting
Ashen skin
A vengeful God
Mauser pistols
Cracked skulls
Mind control
Grocery shopping when you're hungry

Hyperemesis—the excessive vomiting of
    pregnant women
Prominent bones
Being unable to remember if you've had sex
    with someone
Blowflies
The death of Rosencrantz and Guildenstern
Achy, breaky hearts
Show trials
Beautiful old houses worn down by dirt and
    neglect
Soot
Blowfish prepared by an unskilled chef
People who have forgotten how to laugh
The Queen of Spades
Missing your curfew
People who are trampled to death in
    stampedes at rock concerts
Being treated like vermin
Poor relations
Offices without windows
Offices without walls
Conformity
Groups of teenage girls who all dress alike
The pickled body of Vladimir Lenin
Electric shocks
Crucibles
Roommates who don't pay their share of
    the rent
Being ashamed of your father

Mustard gas
Elective surgery
Feeling like a cog in a machine
Ravens quothing "nevermore"
Pistol whipping
Fat cats (metaphorical)
Fat cats (literal)
Golden retrievers with hip dysplasia
Industrial accidents
Saber charges
Handshakes with more than three pumps
Thinking that someone is asleep who is
    actually dead
Believing that the world you know will last
    forever
Long-distance relationships
The glare of sunlight on snow
Crumbling defenses
People who resemble rodents
Getting a tarot card reading that predicts your
    imminent death
TNT
Burials at sea
The explosion of the Mont Blanc
Survivor's guilt
The question: "Would you like me if we
    weren't having sex?"
Getting your kids' favorite Disney songs stuck
    in your head
Seeing more cartoons than real movies

Adults who hold their genitals while waiting in
line to use a public bathroom
Getting a Brazilian wax when you have
your period
Spending Valentine's Day alone with
Ben & Jerry
Big cell phone bills because you get put on
hold all the time
Accidentally pushing your loved one off a
train platform
Cafés with free internet and no outlets
Support groups in church basements
Code Orange terror alert
Sewer explosions
Terrorist attacks on trains
People who don't evacuate when they should
Panic
Veterans' nightmares
Helmet hair
Ransom
Hurricane Camille
Errors due to faulty heuristics
Dread
Smoke detectors with nonworking batteries
Indecision
People who tell you what to do without telling
you why
Poisonous mushrooms
Incontinence
Dissociation

Tunnel vision
High-speed car chases
Midlevel functionaries
Stockholm syndrome
Intifadas
Bad report cards
The fact that more firefighters die on the
    job from heart attacks and strokes than
    from fires
Stakeouts
Convenience store holdups
Post-traumatic stress syndrome in Vietnam
    vets
Shrapnel
Crying in the dark
Fake bearskin rugs in bachelor pads
Groupthink
The illusion of safety in numbers
Evisceration
Pustules
Flying in small planes
Cold mornings when your car won't start
Twins who are forced to dress alike
Drops of pee on toilet seats
Truckers who honk at attractive women
Fastidiousness
Being unable to deposit a check at the ATM
    because you haven't signed the back of it
    and you don't have a pen
Running for the bus and then missing it

Train derailments
Off-track betting
Shoddy engineering
Unknown soldiers
Dead people who can only be identified by
    their dental records
Cracked teacups
The firebombing of Tokyo during World War II
Lost balloons
Having the same name as lots of other people
Needing a kidney
Living somewhere boring
Delayed flights
Discontinued specials
Low-grade, persistent headaches
Having a slow metabolism
Having a low sex drive
Having a high sex drive but no one to have
    sex with
Neglecting to mind the gap
Children quoting advertisements
Squeaky stairs
Children that color all over the walls
Being told to go fuck yourself
Giving up
Breaking the stem of your sunglasses
The exile of the Dalai Lama
The dog pound
Beautiful private golf courses next to
    tenement housing

Tattoo parlors with questionable sanitation
     practices
Rallies that don't actually accomplish anything
Trying to write on a tiny notepad
The higher accidental death rates of left-
     handed people
The hunting of buffalo from trains
The occupation of Poland during World War II
Endless endgames
Realizing you have the wrong order after
     you've gone through the drive-thru
Gasoline poured on people
Children playing at construction sites
Cotton mouth
Cottonmouth snakes
Arriving early to a party
Falling out of a tree
People who act like you're stupid for not
     knowing something they haven't told you
Losing your movie ticket before you go into
     the movie
Drugs slipped into the suitcases of unwitting
     tourists
The pressure to succeed
Dead Christmas trees shedding pine needles
     all over the floor
Career waitresses
Having an advanced degree in a subject that
     has nothing to do with your career
Evening

Being hung up on
Dogs with their vocal chords removed
Listening to other couples fight
People who clean their ears in public
Watching a fish die
Forgetting to take your vitamins
Lumpy noses
Battered women
High school cheerleaders
Fighting about money
Kids repeatedly asking: "Are we there yet?"
Chinchillas in summer
Cousin It
Trying to concentrate
Sunken treasure
Widow's weeds
The smell of kerosene
Boarded-up windows
Boiled cabbage
Small furry animals starving to death in winter
People who tell you their genital warts are just
    skin tags
People who tell you their herpes blisters are
    just pimples
Being tickled
Restraints
Small dogs swept over large waterfalls
The disappearance of Amelia Earhart
Being driven to distraction
Being distracted while driving

Sob stories
Shriveled hot dogs
Friends who love to make you feel like their
     lives are better than yours
Empty afternoons
E-mails updating you on the doings of people
     you don't care about
Kittens stuck in trees
Overconfidence
Intimidation
Advertisements on airplane tray tables
Great artists forced to produce state propaganda
Forgetting your gloves when it's cold out
Going gently into that good night
Leaving your cell phone in a taxi
Getting a call from your gynecologist
Children beaten for making innocent mistakes
Cat scratch fever
Great bands breaking up
The possibility that the Hokey Pokey is not, in
     fact, what it's all about
Children riding tricycles into busy streets
The blue-ringed octopus of the South Seas,
     the most poisonous animal in the world
Fuchsia
Teal
People who describe colors as "fuchsia" or
     "teal"
Skateboarders
Wondering what your life is adding up to

Carcinogenic plastic
"How may I help you?" buttons
People clipping their nails in public
Roommates who steal your food
Having nightmares even after you've bought a
    dream catcher
Bad pot
Dead plants in psychiatrists' offices
Bloodsucking insects
Bloodsucking vampires
Graduation
Declawing cats
Pop radio
Babies crying in movie theaters
Trying to eat a steak without a steak knife
Punctuation mistakes
Bagpipes
Flutists
Mariachi bands
Loud sports bars
Yacht clubs
Plumber's smiles
Bogeys
Double bogeys
Triple bogeys
Tennis faults
Earthquake faults
Particleboard
Missed dunks
Pasteurized processed cheese products

Territorial behavior
Hierarchies
Cubicles
Being described as conventional
Plastic bags washed up on the beach
Pass interference
Pop-ups
Getting junk mail
Sunburn incurred at the tanning salon
Discovering that there is no pot of gold at the
    end of the rainbow
Missing the target
Pound puppies

Mornings

Being short
Being tall
Drop ceilings
Mirrors
Disco balls
Lunchables
Losing one sock in the wash
Having to hang your kids' ugly artwork on
    your fridge
Drink names at Starbucks
Impressionism
Expressionism
Animated animals with enormous eyes
Fossilized remains
Candy that gets stuck in the vending machine
Broken photocopiers
Witness intimidation

Shitting where you eat
Tours of duty
Mood-altering drugs for pets
Bloody crackdowns
The dog days of summer
Writers who produce one great book and then
    never write again
Tongue surgery
Sharpshooters
Self-delusion
Obsessively logical thinking
Nose whistling
People who pronounce "tomato" differently
    than you do
Muzak
Leap year birthdays
Ecoterrorism
Heather Mills
Gigantism
Fish poop
Puffy vests
Public education
Wide-ruled paper
Outmoded technological junk
Subjugation
The firebombing of Dresden
Monica Lewinsky
Famished wolves
Distemper
Free riders

Gonzo
Toasting your marshmallow too long
Not toasting your marshmallow long enough
The suicide of Hunter S. Thompson
Eating at a great restaurant when you're not
    hungry
Missile testing
Themed decor
People who think carob is an acceptable
    substitute for chocolate
Brainwashing
Unconstitutional laws
Phlegm
People who think they can dance
Windburn
The nonexistence of superheroes
People who leave food in communal
    refrigerators for months
People who don't wash their dishes at work
Memos
Children who shoot paintballs at other
    people's houses
Saddle sweat
Trying to find a babysitter at the last minute
Know-it-alls
Put-downs
Fetid stinkpits
Going on vacation and forgetting your
    makeup bag
Bad tippers

People who go through CDs at the record
store and don't put them back in
alphabetical order
People who try on clothes and leave them all
over the dressing room floor
Brain drain
Having no idea which foods are actually bad
for you or good for you anymore
Beauty pageant contestants whose careers are
ruined by racy photos
Wood lice
Being attacked by birds
Cell doors slamming shut
Inglorious bastards
Split lips
Overflowing slop buckets
Clothing that takes more than five minutes to
remove
Interrogations
Sadistic wardens
Dripping water
Wall-to-wall carpeting
Hospitals that smell like disinfectant
Greasepaper
Strumpets
Othello's handkerchief
Chairs bolted to the floor
Naked lightbulbs
Pond scum
Men who undress women with their eyes

Being told to have a good day by indescribably
   depressed grocery store clerks
Slugs
Shuffling off this mortal coil
Nightsticks
Sledgehammers
Death warrants
Sailing races that end in drowning
Toddlers with enormous heads
Valet parking for tricycles
Sallow skin
Thick skulls
Breech births
Pellagra—a vitamin deficiency that causes
   diarrhea and eventual dementia
Yellow-bellied cowards
Rotten potatoes
Biblical quotations incorporated into foreplay
Arrow wounds
Teenage girls whose only ambition is to get
   breast implants
Dislocated shoulders
Tolling bells
Walking into a room in which you are being
   discussed
Eyes swollen shut
Dried blood
Police frisking that devolves into sodomy
People who think God hates their enemies
Chipped teeth

Men who blame their impotence on their lovers
Being crushed by a Murphy bed
Badly written sex scenes
Parts of the world in which your religion is
    hazardous to your health
Bar brawls
Paymasters
Labor camps
Saddlebags
The fact that Britney Spears' uneaten French
    toast was sold on eBay
Searches for meaning in the universe that end
    at the local bar
The bleak midwinter
Broken lightbulbs that you can't unscrew
    without cutting yourself
The thought of Mother Teresa in a swimsuit
People who answer yes or no questions with
    cryptic aphorisms about sand and eternity
Self-abasement
Losing your keys
Fake pearls
Ass combs
Rutabagas
Nights on which the cult leader chooses
    your wife
Rodent teeth
Surgeons with slow learning curves
Invented sexual exploits
Not really knowing what "Free Tibet" means

People who think Aunt Jemima was a civil
  rights leader
Contaminated water
Celebrities who are photographed with great
  books but never read them
Damp, miserable huts
Slit throats
Augusto Pinochet—a brutal Chilean dictator
Goose-stepping soldiers
Persistent boors
Disemboweled dogs
Informers
Men killed by their own booby traps
Friends who don't let you get a word in edgewise
Idealists
Belching chimneys
Getting splashed by a taxi
Skinned knees
Pet snakes that eat their owners
Ominous growls
Being grounded
Eating paste
Bottomless pits
People who talk about celebrities as if
  they're friends
Half-starved horses
Needing to obtain a restraining order
Bombed cathedrals
Dying for nothing
The hygiene habits of hillbillies

Mistaking a headache for a brain tumor
Mistaking a brain tumor for a headache
People with contagious viruses on crowded
    flights
People with a different wildly implausible
    excuse each time they're late
People with the same wildly implausible
    excuse each time they're late
Airlines that refuse to pay for your hotel after
    canceling your flight
Being hit with a snowball
Bits of brown, rotting flesh
Inuit babies eaten by wolves
Native Americans forced onto reservations
Doctors who perform unnecessary but
    lucrative procedures
Marrying an ax murderer
Composers remembered by posterity for
    thirty seconds of their work
Dating a married man
Paper trails
Pathological liars
People who refer to their children as "the
    consequences of their choices"
Being robbed by a prostitute
Obsessive exes
The fading hope of reconciliation
Daggers hidden in cloaks
People whose dieting strategy is to refer to
    themselves as "the cow"

Failing to notice blatant signs that your date is attracted to you and thus not getting laid

Being told: "I can't sleep with you until I'm drunker"

Watching the pained facial expressions of someone reading your writing who doesn't know it's your writing

Pickup artists

Having a drink spilled on you accidentally

Having a drink spilled on you on purpose

Women who refer to their infant son as "the only decent man in my life"

Hair plugs

Aspartame

Women killed for sexual misconduct

Getting your shirt caught in your zipper

Getting your penis caught in your zipper

Really old cat litter

Going to the emergency room

African driver ants

People who spend more time with their cars than their families

Not knowing how to perform the Heimlich maneuver

Having your credit card declined

People who complain about their spacious, beautiful homes

Weak handshakes

The sudden emergence of unexpected obstacles

Parting salvos

Forgetting your significant other's birthday
Your significant other forgetting your birthday
Hemorrhoidectomies
Foods with more additives than ingredients
Trying to stop a wedding
Life insurance salesmen
Sturm und drang
Children dressed in burlap sacks
Cattle cars
Old football injuries
Nineteenth century industrialists indifferent
    to the plight of those on whom their
    fortune depended
Crow's feet
Being summarily dismissed
Drunken bets that end in marriage
Running into your children while dining with
    your extramarital lover
People who look happy all the time
Men who call their girlfriend's dad "Dude"
Algae in swimming pools
Concussions
Seedy, depressing strip clubs
Profiteering
The fact that more people are familiar with Sam
    Adams as a beer than as a historical figure
Mistaking an orgasm for a seizure
Mistaking a seizure for an orgasm
Sweating the small stuff
Ugly people reading fashion magazines

The link between preservatives and
    hyperactivity
People who try to stick their tongue down
    your throat
Having to choose between death and dishonor
Denying a crime you're in the process of
    committing
Suicidal ignorance
Sodium nitrite
Money that you thought was a loan and your
    child thought was a gift
Policemen who want their wives to address
    them as "Officer"
Rigor mortis
Cats put in dishwashers
Japanese teenagers who spend all their time
    in cyberspace
Paralyzing social anxiety
The fact that humans produce almost a liter of
    gas daily
Borscht
Burkina Faso, which has the lowest literacy
    rate in the world (12.8 percent)
Getting caught off guard
Terrifyingly enlarged photos
Being stabbed with a letter opener
Broken ribs
Maritime law
Being forced to walk the plank
Kindness motivated by guilt

Gonococcus—the bacteria that causes
   gonorrhea
Whip-cracking
People who compare themselves to Christ
   without a trace of irony
Aphasia
Feminists who don't shave their armpits
Reductive scientific explanations of beautiful
   sunsets
Being told to shove something up your ass
Children who dump out the entire contents of
   their mothers' handbags
Not feeling all that sad when your
   grandmother dies
Cars wrapped around trees
Cows with only three stomachs
Slit wrists in warm water
Failing the bar exam
The Battle of Guernica
Greek gods who miss being worshipped
Shootings in malls
Sitting through all of Wagner's *Die Walküre*
The scum of the earth
Sexual deviants
Performances of Barber's *Adagio for Strings* to
   commemorate national tragedies
Money-grubbers
Majorettes
Beanie Babies
Fanny packs

Doctors who jump to conclusions
Screaming fans
Celebrity entourages
Mistaking walls for doors
Losing your child in a department store
Having your head shoved into a bucket
Nerds with violent revenge fantasies
Brendan Frasier
Feeling like you're running on a hamster
wheel
Alveolar capillary dysplasia
Cigarette advertisements
Hitting your head on the diving board
Baby fat
Mothers who spend child support money on
themselves
Iwo Jima
Dalliances
The paralysis of Christopher Reeve
Losing the remote in the couch cushions
Rafael Leonidas Trujillo Molina—assassinated
dictator of the Dominican Republic
Being dumped because your boyfriend finds
you depressing
Dogs that sleep in the same bed as their owners
Dirtbags
Sigmoidoscopy
Breast reduction surgery
Having an "off" year
Sidewinding adders

Anti-gay activists caught with male prostitutes
Beer bellies
Once-beautiful women who age badly
Media moguls
Feeling guilty for not calling your parents
    often enough
Teenagers who dig up corpses and use the
    skulls to smoke pot
Airbrushing
Being the first one in your family to get
    divorced
Shopping sprees in Paris
The tip of the iceberg
Chicken abuse by KFC
Websites that purport to tell you how old
    you'll be when you die
Ruffled feathers
Patsy Ramsey, who died before she could be
    vindicated for her daughter's murder
Breach of contract
Not being allowed to see your kids
Drug-laced Halloween candy
Getting arrested for having sex in public
Getting arrested and thrown in jail for several
    years for having sex in public in an Arab
    country
Black lung disease
Overpaid CEOs
Underpaid workers
Risky investments

The fact that eighteen-year-olds are allowed to
    go to war but not allowed to drink
Stonewalling
Uninsured cancer patients
Sweetheart deals
The 18,000 Americans who die each year
    because they can't afford heath care
Outright fabrications
Irrational escalation—a phenomenon whereby
    people continue pouring time and energy
    into a pointless project because of the time
    and energy they previously invested in it
Gaza prison, the world's largest prison with
    1.5 million inmates
"Undesirables"
Beehive hairdos
Trying to alter a tattoo of your ex's name
Laid-off journalists
Uninspected products from China
Flights that leave at 6 A.M.
Counting the days until your next vacation
Trade imbalances
The 58,000 Americans who die annually due
    to workplace diseases and traumas
Predatory lending practices
Fine print
The thousands of Chinese people who lost
    their homes with no reimbursement so the
    Chinese government could make way for
    the Olympics

IVs

Embargoes

Wheezing

Little girls who are told to be ladylike

Watercress finger sandwiches

Repetitive stress injuries

The fact that more toxic dumps are found in
    poor neighborhoods

The failure of the war on drugs

Gerrymandering

Enron

Hidden mutual fund fees

Quagmires

Anaphylactic shock

Lost traditions

Martial law

Class-action lawsuits

The possibility of World War III

Chemical weapons

Kowtowing

Senator Larry Craig

Mock humility

Chickening out

Mastectomies

Electrolysis

Female pattern baldness

Life-threatening peanut allergies

Rusty monkey bars

Temp jobs

Tattletales

Cheesy wedding vows
Three strikes
Trying to get a kite airborne
Killing time
The straw that breaks the camel's back
Scott Peterson
The link between lung ailments and
    microwave popcorn
Men who think women talk with their breasts
    instead of their mouths
Dirty handkerchiefs
Saggy pecs
Trying to use chopsticks when you don't
    know how
Nervous laughter
Scrawny legs
Going into combat
Crybabies
O. J. Simpson
Jumping jacks
Tumbleweeds
Bags of shit set on fire
Ice ages
Emotional cheating
Spiderwebs in corners of the ceiling you
    can't reach
Having to wear a cast
Bullhorns
Trying to find your way around an
    unfamiliar city

Critical condition
Avocado-colored paint
Gary Condit
Backpedaling
Not having rhythm
Buying tampons
Men who expose themselves to children
Weeping and gnashing of teeth
Young children left alone
Raffi
Unmarried women with multiple cats
Believing you deserve to be happier
Someone else reading your diary
Bald-faced lies
Packing
Unpacking
Girls with mothers who are more beautiful
    than they are
Other people living in your childhood home
Mountain highways with no guard rails
Being unable to fit into your wedding dress
Roommates who play the saxophone
Wet paint
Corporate break rooms
Foot-and-mouth disease
Losing an important client
Meaningless details
Sex with interns
People who commute to work by helicopter
Disappointing honeymoons

Being held hostage by Colombian rebels
People who refer to sex as "intercourse"
Divorcing and remarrying the same person
    multiple times
Tactlessness
Spoilsports
Hospital visits
Angina
Wigs
Frumpiness
People who use the word "pecker"
Intensive care
Empty beer cans
Doing penance
Hissy fits
Dying without a will
Walking on eggshells (metaphorically)
Walking on eggshells (literally)
Miracle cures that are neither miraculous nor
    curative
The smell of air freshener
Being spied on in the shower through the
    bathroom skylight
Not knowing how to pronounce "açai"
Commercials for anti-acne products that show
    disgusting close-ups of pimples
Ugly ducklings that never turn into swans
Bright blue cocktails
Being chased by loan sharks
Leaving the sprinkler on too long

Greasy hair
Being in labor for a long time
Trying to take a baby shopping
Complacency
Getting stuck in a dress you're trying on
Glandular fever
Dogs with broken legs
Parachutes that fail to open
Giving money to people before realizing
    they're not actually homeless
Vulnerability
Gas pains
Secret smokers
Interviews with co-op boards
Army wives whose husbands are at war
Soil degradation
Sensitive teeth
Forgetting to do breast self-exams
Seborrheic keratoses—brown wart-like
    growths on skin
Twitches
Joan Rivers
Neck surgery
Movie stars appearing on Broadway
Lysosomal storage disorders
Hearses
Getting chlorine up your nose
Hair that turns green from pool water
Getting pieces of popcorn stuck in between
    your teeth

Rotten tuna fish
Muckrakers
Cluster bombs
Lead contamination in urban gardens
Journalists who rely on secondary sources
Roadside improvised explosive devices
Smoking in children's movies
Hand grenades
The fact that theme parks, casinos, and
  prisons are among the fastest-growing
  American businesses
Apologists
Criminal negligence
How little most Americans know about the
  rest of the world
Trophy wives
Hostile takeovers
Houses bulldozed to make way for
  superhighways
The fall of Icarus
Unscrupulous bounty hunters who arrest
  innocent people for cash
Bile
Iraqi civilian casualties
Congressional "pork"
Sedition
Unreliable price estimates
Shoestring budgets
Rollover crashes
Criminal misconduct

The fact that African-American women are
thirteen times more likely than white
women to be diagnosed with HIV
Deteriorating coral reefs
Synthetic nitrogen fertilizers in the Gulf of
Mexico
Metastases
The things people are forced to eat on *Fear
Factor*
Neighbor children who steal flowers from
your yard
Rigid beliefs
Trying to put sunscreen on your own back
The commercialization of cancer
Being thrown into a swimming pool with your
clothes on
People who are constantly tap dancing
Studies showing that Type A personalities have
more than twice as many heart attacks
Communication breakdowns
Looking at diagrams of the reproductive system
Daddy longlegs spiders
Health class
Screeching tires
Pleurisy—a painful inflammation of the cavity
surrounding the lungs
Loose threads
Fighting with your mom
Fighting with your dad
Waking up covered with sweat

Pity
Resignation
People who get engaged after dating for only
    a few weeks
Oxygen tanks
Instant coffee
Foods with suspiciously long shelf lives
Mail addressed to dead people
Infinity
People with nicer houses than you
Computers that make strange buzzing noises
People who don't call you back
Children born without thigh bones
Progeria—a rare condition that accelerates
    the physical aspects of aging
Answering yes to most of the questions on the
    "Are you an alcoholic?" checklist
Late-night commercials that make you want
    food from restaurants that aren't open
Missed opportunities
Planned obsolescence
Corporate raiders
Circling vultures
Incompetent coxswains
The Dred Scott case
Bent nails
Marilyn Monroe
Marilyn Manson
Charles Manson
People who whistle at waiters like they're dogs

Choosing
a coffin

Being unable to access your e-mail due to a
temporary problem with your account
Wells running dry (literally)
Wells running dry (metaphorically)
The silent treatment
People who act like they're still in high school
People who act like they're still in elementary
school
Being treated like dirt
Cronyism
The bursting of the dot-com bubble
Illegal offshore accounts
Conflicts of interest
Malfeasance
Survival of the fittest
Marketing targeted at children
Industrial espionage
Slack packaging—products sold in boxes that
are not completely full
Cell phones ringing in church
Classes taught by TAs
Blocked toilets in public bathrooms
People who believe their crappy childhoods
exempt them from treating others well
Accidentally hammering your fingers
Accidentally hammering someone else's
fingers
Motorcycle crashes
"Missed connections" postings on Craigslist
that are never about you

Subway stations without air conditioning in
    summer
College students who have never been kissed
Minotaurs
Flipping burgers
Making copies for a living
Snot-nosed kids
Asparagus ice cream
People who get onto trains before letting
    others get off
Britney Spears' perfumes
Dead men walking
The Aryan Brotherhood
Folsom Prison
San Quentin
Repairs made by unlicensed handymen
Stained couch cushions
Leaking ceilings
Being escorted out of your office by security
Thunderstorms on camping trips
Brokers who talk too fast
Headless dolls
Headless horsemen
Cats that attack strangers
Tickets for drinking in public
The stamp tax
Women with ex-boyfriends who are
    convicted felons
Living with your grandparents
Lawn flamingos

The Reign of Terror

Robespierre

The British colonization of India

The assassination of Archduke Francis
Ferdinand

Failed attempts at disarmament

General Franco

Molotov cocktails

Lee Harvey Oswald

John Wilkes Booth

Optic neuritis

The rite of janhar, in which Indian men in the
Middle Ages burned their wives and children
and then went forth to meet their death

The Opium Wars

The rape of Nanjing

Corrupt regents

Indoctrination

The Korean War

One-crop economies

One-party states

Civil war in Angola

Sleeping sickness

The forcing of Russian peasants into
collectivist farms in the 1930s

Low birth rates

High birth rates

Hara-kiri—a famous form of Japanese ritual
suicide

Mata Hari—a famous spy

The rising Consumer Price Index

Putting lipstick on a pig

Little boys who pull the wings off crickets

Lent

People who think everyone with HIV is gay

People who think everyone who's gay has HIV

Classes on subjects you don't care about

Chewing gum that loses flavor immediately

The stony soil of New England

The War of Spanish Succession

Lot's wife

Tarring and feathering

Ants at a picnic

The "Black Friday" gold conspiracy

Short-term memory loss

Long-term memory loss

Unfounded speculation

Journalists who make up facts

Studies showing that bone-building drugs
    may actually weaken bones

Clay feet

Stress fractures

Consultations with surgeons

Jokes about various people and/or animals
    walking into bars

Lyme disease

Going to school on the "short bus"

Landslides

The 1998 Yangtze River floods, which left 14
    million Chinese people homeless

Global health emergencies

Solar flares

Giving in to temptation

Advertisements that encourage giving in to
temptation

Damage control

Abnormal pupillary reflexes

Hypoxia

Malware

Intracranial pressure

The Great Lisbon Earthquake of 1755

Sexual harassment and rape of female U.S.
soldiers in Iraq

Anti-acne products that dry out your skin and
still leave you with acne

Not getting thank-you notes for gifts you've sent

Being bedridden

Direct-to-video movies

Dead languages

Politicians who reverse their positions on
issues once they get elected

Cover-ups

Watergate

Waterloo

All the great bands you've never heard of

Impulse buying

Needing a haircut

Sodom

Gomorrah

Solitary lights in office building windows

Joggers wearing black on busy roads at night

Backing over your trashcan in the driveway

Backing over your toddler in the driveway

Not being allowed to turn right on red

Not being allowed to make a U-turn

People who lock their car doors only when
driving through minority neighborhoods

The smell of warm chocolate chip cookies
when you're dieting

Movies about hookers with hearts of gold

Couples therapy

Food as reward

Food as punishment

Power struggles

Robert Mugabe—president of Zimbabwe

Realizing something is expired after you've
bought it

Cyclists on steroids

Rising prices for small cars

Junk bonds

Repenting at leisure

Contaminated blood

The fact that the U.S. spends twice as much
per person on health care as other
industrialized countries, but comes in
last place in preventing deaths through
medical care

White dwarfs

Red giants

Knickknacks

Clicking your heels together three times but
    not ending up back in Kansas
Paying thousands of dollars for art that turns
    out to be fake
Osama bin Laden
The devastation of the Native American
    population by European diseases
Playing with fire
Oliver North—a Reagan-era official involved
    in the sale of weapons to Iran
Death squads
Jesuit priests murdered in El Salvador
Wreckage
Oil slicks
Fireballs
Smoke from factory chimneys
White knuckle landings
Bodies that are never found
Planes that fly into mountains
The massacre at Sand Creek
The Conscription Act of 1863, which allowed
    wealthy draftees to buy their way out of
    the draft for $300
Chokedamp, a mixture of oxygen-deficient
    gases that causes suffocation
Blasting powder accidents
Medieval zealots
The London Fire of 1666
Accidentally booking a vacation to a tropical
    island during its rainy season

Saint Vitus' Dance
Cyclones
Hungry furnaces
Squalor
Squalling
Squalls
Runny mascara
Toxic waste
Chain-link fences
Cages
Machines
Billboards
Delays
Bad parties
Not being able to dance
Not hitting the ball
Barney
Walt Disney
Psychopharmacology
Cigarettes
Bad coffee
Glitter
Rainbows
Shag carpeting
Linoleum
Wasted food
Kids who eat too much sugar
Paper jams
Rising stamp prices
Moth holes

Junk drawers

School uniforms

Being poked by your bra's underwire

Swallowing a bug

Trans fats

Polka dots

Uncomfortable chairs

Scratched corneas

Buying babies

White patent leather shoes

Children whose ambition in life is to be class
president

Weirdly small ears

Blue-haired old ladies

People who cry after sex

People who cry during sex

Rebellious teenagers sent to military school

Pug noses

Greasy egg rolls

Public displays of affection

Public displays of repulsion

Pants that make you look fat

People who tell you that the pants that make
you look fat don't make you look fat

People who go ahead and admit that the pants
make you look fat

Graduation speeches that quote from *Oh, the
Places You'll Go* by Dr. Seuss

Graduation speeches that quote from "The
Road Not Taken" by Robert Frost

Shame
Shamelessness
Ineffective love potions
Bloodshot eyes
Odes on Grecian urns
Negative campaign ads
Protozoa
Not getting into your first choice college
Not getting into your last choice college
Hunchbacks
Pepto-Bismol pink
Jitters
Surgically enhanced necks
Walkers
Windbreakers
Breaking wind
Torn rotator cuffs
Trying to concentrate while stoned
Teachers who are fired for sexually abusing
    students
Embarrassing middle names
Movies that glamorize teen pregnancy
Movies that demonize teen pregnancy
Having bad love poems written about you
Writing bad love poems about someone else
Stretched-out waistbands
Rules and regulations
Carpal tunnel syndrome
Ganglion cysts
Inaccurate surveys

Finding out how many calories are in your
favorite foods
Children who think their dead pets are
coming back someday
Snowballing lies
Houses of cards
False labor
Festering wounds
Sciatica
Songs that remind you of your ex
Forgetting the combination to your bike lock
Anatomically correct children's toys
Mongrels
Arterial dissection
Women who put on makeup to go to the gym
Great power without great responsibility
Packages lost in the mail
Trade deficits
High maintenance girls
Enormous executive compensation packages
Recipes that require fancy kitchen equipment
Fatal attraction
Runaway trucks
Runaway bunnies
Finding out someone else has already written
the book you want to write
Your favorite singer getting booted off
American Idol
Having your ex on all your emergency contact
forms

Overindulgent grandparents
The children of divorced parents
Cram sessions
Pantsuits
Scratchy wool tights
People with country houses
Vanity sizing
Bulging disks
The cost of Japanese hair straightening
    treatments
Wax figures that look more lifelike than the
    celebrities they're based on
The fact that Botox actually stands for
    "botulinum toxin"
Teens with their parents' credit cards
Teens with their own credit cards
Glass houses
Postal workers going postal
Teenagers who think Kerouac's *On the Road*
    is the key to the meaning of life
Inadvertently starring in a scandalous
    YouTube video
Crocs
Mea culpas
Not being able to sit together at the movies
Politicians who misread their teleprompters
Sand flies
Roadside mine searches
Stuffed shirts
Stuffed bras

The lack of safe drinking water for troops in Iraq

Feeling as if you're missing out on something

Children raised by their nannies

Preschool waiting lists

Tofu dogs

Flower print Laura Ashley dresses

Cold fish (metaphorical)

Cold fish (literal)

Trying to convince yourself something is
shabby chic when it's really just shabby

People who pick their teeth in public

Group hugs

Hickeys

Puddles

Paying $8 for popcorn at the movies

Having the salad dressing arrive on top of
your salad when it was supposed to arrive
on the side

Pants splitting up the ass seam

Buying rotten produce and not noticing until
you get home

Broken eggs in the carton

Broken eggs on the floor

Sand castles washing away

Novels that use sand castles washing away as
a metaphor

Having to repeat yourself

Not screwing on the lid of your water bottle
tightly enough and soaking everything in
your bag

Angst
Waiting all day for the cable guy
Waiting all month for the cable guy
Being unable to figure out which Tupperware
    lid fits on your sandwich container
Having to switch containers and losing half the
    contents of your sandwich in the transfer
Roommates who incessantly hit the snooze
    button
Stepping on a hot sidewalk with bare feet
Egomaniac directors
Watery scrambled eggs
Dead pigeons
People who hang naked photographs of
    themselves as art
Refuse in the gutter
Water-stained ceilings
Riding a bike up a steep hill
Glasses with lipstick marks
Owning one of the ten most-stolen cars:
    Honda Civic
    Honda Accord
    Toyota Camry
    Ford F-150
    Chevrolet C/K 1500
    Acura Integra
    Dodge Ram Pickup
    Nissan Sentra
    Toyota Pickup
    Toyota Corolla

Bicycle shorts
Gargoyles
Bra straps falling off your shoulders
Pod people
Fights with bouncers
Advertisements disguised as magazine articles
Not knowing your measurements
Ominous knocks on the door when you're
    home alone
Leather pants
Anomie
Children who enjoy torturing animals
The criminally insane
Dystopias
Skullduggery
Homesickness
Cold dead hands
Slobodan Milošević
The taste of moonshine
Hardscrabble mountain towns
Creeks filled with snakes
Degradation
Loaded dice
Dirt floors
Dyspepsia
Suppurating sores
Babies eaten by tigers
Needing to shave
The taste of cough medicine
Having to say you're sorry

Sweeping the floor
Not sweeping the floor
Senility
The end of your lunch hour
Duplicity
Restaurants where the gratuity is included
and the service is terrible
Finding the perfect pair of pants in the
wrong size
Barbarians
Muscle tension
Pollen
Frost
Septic wounds
Interest on loans
The Bay of Pigs
Being unjustly criticized
Being justly criticized
Old boys' clubs
Admitting you've made a mistake
Hogwash
Boundary disputes
Ambiguity
Getting what you deserve
Not getting what you deserve
Furniture covered in plastic
Getting lost when you're already late
Sewers
Toddlers who throw food on the floor
Wasted lives

Running out of gas
Farting
Politics
The national debt
Engine trouble
Splinters
Splinter cells
Knee replacements
The Irish potato famine
Fouls
Down payments
Meth mouth—loss of teeth from long-term
    crystal meth use
Impermanence
Dungeons
Dragons
Dungeons & Dragons
The fact that there's no such thing as a
    free lunch
Blizzards
Air raids
Stalling out
The draft
The file on you that may exist in some
    government office somewhere
Rot
Debts
November rain
Murder weapons
Your posture

Power outages
Inertia
Couch potatoes
Winter clothes
Fishtailing
Ships smashed on rocks
Sunburn
Socks that don't stay up
The Old Testament God
People who act like martyrs
People who really are martyrs
Chum
Lying to your parents
Lying to your children
Outhouses
Bad sex
Bathing suit shopping
Buttoning your shirt one button off
Accidentally drinking household cleaning
    products
Condescension
Shipwrecks
Cleaning out the food processor
Getting shots
Getting shot
Drunk people when you're sober
Sober people when you're drunk
People who will never be as happy as they
    were in high school
Sneakers that smell even after washing

Explosive
diarrhea

Paint drips on the rug
Home shows that recommend nine months of
    decorating in thirty minutes
Men who alternate the same two suits for five
    years straight
Accidentally tucking your skirt into your
    underwear
The smell of hog pens
Hard times
Child labor
Wobbly chairs
Growing up
Dysentery
Chores
Friendly fire
The Battle of Shiloh
Mechanical error
Human error
Foxholes
Stringy hair
Declining amphibian populations, an indicator
    of environmental distress
The odor of corpses
Leaving your curling iron on and starting a fire
Thirst
Buck teeth
Hitting your tailbone
Muddy boots on clean floors
Not having a spare tire
Dust bunnies

Getting lemon juice in your eye
Chopping onions
Burnt food
Obnoxious radio personalities
People who sing loudly and out of tune
Swimmer's itch
Fruit flies
Sand in your shoes
Losing your passport abroad
Laugh lines
The Book of Revelations
The dog getting out
Getting transferred
Burning yourself while ironing
Running out of hot water in the shower
The dog eating your homework
The link between cell phone use and male
    infertility
Getting an MRI
Wrinkles in your clothes
Wrinkles in your face
Being cold
Locking your keys in the car
Finding a Band-Aid in your food
Fire drills
Incriminating photographs
Not being taken seriously
Being underestimated
Pit stains
Mosquito bites

Forty-year-old virgins
Not knowing how to spell
Call center personnel who don't speak English
Stepping on gum
Missing your favorite TV show
Hearing the score before seeing the game
The stock market
Downsizing
Missing the beginning of a movie
Traffic jams due to rubbernecking
Smoky bars
Kidnapping
The atomic bomb
Segregation
Broken hair ties
Attending the wedding of someone you're in
    love with
Dictators
Rotten bananas
Carjacking
Being an only child
Being an oldest child
Being a middle child
Being a youngest child
Burning your tongue on hot coffee
Your biological clock
Deforestation
Shoplifting
Invented memoirs
The Tet Offensive

Waiting in line at clubs

Getting to the front of the line, but not being cool enough to get in

Sleazeballs

Cheeseballs

People who electrocute themselves by using a hair dryer in the bathtub

Double digit IQs

Loving someone more than they love you

The 11 million orphans in Africa

Paparazzi

Assault

Countries without freedom of the press

Karl Rove

Fourteen-year-olds in sexy outfits

The return of '80s fashion

The return of '80s movie stars

Heidi Montag

Spencer Pratt

Public opinion

Hallucinations

Other people's narcissism

Your own narcissism

Hidden cameras

The assassination of John F. Kennedy

Waking up from unsettling dreams to find yourself transformed into a giant cockroach

Drug addicts

Fear itself

Bronchitis

Actors who decide they want to write
Models who decide they want to act
Finding out at the end of a meeting that you
    have spinach stuck in your teeth
Queen bees
Nits
Bad reviews of good movies
Good reviews of bad movies
Kim Jong Il
Numerology
Being unprepared
People who jump off the Golden Gate Bridge
People kissing on street corners
Agents
Being told what to do
Spending too much on other people's weddings
Spending too much on your own wedding
Getting in a car crash while wearing dirty
    underwear
Estranged siblings
Losing your driver's license
Train wrecks (literal)
Train wrecks (metaphorical)
Carpenter bees
People who talk about you in a foreign
    language and assume you don't understand
Alcoholic parents
Putting yourself on a budget
Dead baby birds
Indecent exposure

Working with someone who doesn't shower
Burnt toast
People who are famous for no reason
Hookers who ply their trade in public parks
Getting to the end of a really good book
Afghanistan
Earthquakes
Getting kicked out of a bar
Carrying last season's handbag
Not having a good candidate to vote for
Failing a class
Falling off your bike
Being the only one of your friends who's single
Serfs
Multicar pileups
Tsunamis
Cold water in the shower
Waiting
Doctors who are continually running late
Stale bread
Bumping your head on the cupboard door
Running out of envelopes when you need to
    mail something
Coming out from under anesthesia
Being outside in the rain
Scratched leather
Parking tickets
Stupid human tricks
Bouncers
Getting sued

Not getting flowers on Valentine's Day
Being on a roller coaster when someone vomits
Stitches
The Foot Clan
Putting your tongue on metal in the winter
Rust
Losing your wireless signal
Getting stuck behind a school bus
Parking in Manhattan
Talking to someone who has an enormous zit
Dirty diapers
Elevator malfunctions
Your mother-in-law
Dropping your ice cream cone
Bird shit on your windshield
Getting up early
Getting in your car in the summer
Elderly drivers
Spilled beer
Putting all of your eggs in one basket and then
    dropping the basket
Paper cuts
Stubbing your toe
Customer service jobs
Having curly hair
Having straight hair
Insects that fly up into the light fixture and
    die there
Ugliness
Time running out

Rain on your wedding day
A free ride when you've already paid
The good advice that you just didn't take
Poverty
Adult acne
Not knowing what you want to do when you
    grow up
The college admissions process
Golfer's elbow
Dirty cars
Leaving your cell phone at home
Hot flashes
The Fall of Saigon
Sitting on an airport runway for hours
Highway tolls
Loud noises
Roommates
Someone hitting your parked car
Not having school canceled when it snows
Falling
Dull scissors
Trying to spread cold butter on soft bread
Seagulls
Razor burn
Getting blood taken
Finding a dead fish in your fish tank
Road trips with people who refuse to stop for
    bathroom breaks
Road trips with people who constantly want to
    stop for bathroom breaks

Political correctness
President George W. Bush
Hunger
Errands
Chronic fatigue syndrome
Birds eating your garden
The fact that the people who can afford to travel
    are generally the ones who don't appreciate it
Writing a dissertation
The DMV
Stray peppercorns wedged in your molars
Overhearing private cell phone conversations
    where someone is getting dumped
Wondering if high school students think
    you're cool
Slush on the sidewalks for weeks after it snows
Not giving money to homeless people and
    then feeling guilty about it
Just missing the subway
Having your shopping cart taken by
    somebody else
Biting your tongue (literally)
Biting your tongue (metaphorically)
Waiting in line at airport security
Bad endings
Clogged drains
Fibromyalgia
Second place
Sulfurous fumes seeping from volcanoes
Essay questions

Missing a basket
The Cigarette Smoking Man
Slamming your hand in the car door
Finding a hair in your food
Finding a rat in your bottle of soda
Receiving an ugly engagement ring
Receiving an ugly engagement ring from an
    ugly person
Writing thank-you notes
Broken mufflers
Obligatory invites
Millions of empty water bottles rotting in
    landfills
Meeting people for the first time at your wedding
Teratogenic substances, which cause birth
    defects in babies
Hothouse tomatoes
Accidentally leaving your children at the
    grocery store
Sending out résumés
Stained sheets
Your credit score
Disaster victims
Attention deficit disorder
The rampant overdiagnosis of attention
    deficit disorder
Women who dress like strippers
Sadism
Masochism
Sadomasochism

Ice cream trucks that actually sell drugs
Asthma
Jimbo, Dolph, and Kearney
Seasonal affective disorder
The Hamptons
Neurotics
Living in an apartment building with no elevator
The foster care system
Penn Station
Conspicuous consumption
Measles
Mumps
Rubella
Sauron
Voting in Florida
Aspic
Inappropriate jokes
Belly fat
Varicose veins
The obituary section
Sales tax
Colombian warlords
Snuff
Snuff films
Cookie-cutter suburban developments
Human trafficking
The taste of Manischewitz
Eliot Spitzer
Gang violence
Wildfires in California

Deportation
Extramarital affairs
Metal detectors in public schools
Lobbyists
Utility bills
Drivers who fall asleep behind the wheel
The old ball and chain
The U.S. refusal to ratify the Kyoto Protocol,
    which would reduce greenhouse gas
    emissions
Limbo
Being neither fish nor fowl
Demon spawn
Cruelty to animals
Silverfish
Having beautiful friends
Jewish guilt
Pinkeye
Gout
Mass mailings
Black widow spiders
The possibility of losing your home
Surfing accidents
Extortion
Real estate developers
Sexism
Attrition
Rubble
Skeletor
Jeans shopping

Rapacious appetites
Waste
Thousand-dollar haircuts
The unlikelihood that the Oscar acceptance
 speech you practice in the shower will ever
 be put to use
Trying to get in shape for bathing suit season
Failing to get in shape for bathing suit season
Celebrities who get DUIs before they're old
 enough to drink
People who get arrested for crimes they didn't
 commit
People who don't get arrested for crimes they
 did commit
Jobs without health benefits
Losing money at a casino
Winning money at a casino, but then losing it
 all again
Catcalls
The feudal system
Alimony
Puppy mills
Being pressured to have children
Pink slips
Roller-coaster accidents
Procrastination
Junkies
Boring conversations
Aliens
Perfectionism

Vince McMahon, chairman of World
Wrestling Entertainment
The self-help section
Clothes you bought months ago but have
never worn
Detours
Monomania
Mononucleosis
Attack dogs
Sleep deprivation
The defense department
Secrecy
Naomi Campbell's treatment of her assistants
Unplanned pregnancies
Audits
Bad oysters
Weather forecasts that predict rain all week
Pincers
Bankruptcy
Monsters that live under the bed
Gas leaks
Monogamy
Polygamy
Paradox
Anemia
Type 1 diabetes
Type 2 diabetes
Saving for retirement
Not saving for retirement
Taking care of your parents

Morons
Ageism
Callousness
Callouses
The Battle of Antietam
Repo men
Dark and stormy nights
Binge eating
Hard luck stories
Stress hormones
Baggage (literal)
Baggage (metaphorical)
The lack of emphasis on critical thinking in
    the public schools
Touching a hot stove
Carpetbaggers
Gambling addictions
Sisyphus
Lex Luthor
The thirteenth floor
Reaping what you sow
Scandals involving nude photos of teenage
    celebrities
Breaking dishes
Domestic violence
Going to the gynecologist
Trying to quit smoking
Granny panties
Park Slope playgrounds
Hateful English teachers

Semiotics

Confessions

People who act like they're going to kiss your
cheek and then kiss your mouth

People who act like they're going to kiss your
mouth and then kiss your cheek

Wine coolers

Indifference

Saltine crackers

Rough seas

Piggy from *Lord of the Flies*

Scarlet letters

Stomachaches

Terrell Owens

Drew Rosenhaus, Terrell Owens' agent

The Mummy

Antimacassars

Frozen chicken potpies

Failed novelists who end up working as
technical copywriters

Being spit on from a great height

Being unable to say no

Being in the closet

Inconsistencies

Viral video hoaxes

Spiritual deserts

Carrying water for miles

Countries ranked low on the U.N. Human
Development Index

Alternate-side parking regulations

Mothers who claim they're not hungry in
    order to feed their children
Unresolved nuclear talks
Government takeovers of private businesses
Visa problems
Countries that are unfriendly to foreigners
Public executions
Roadside checkpoints
Going overboard (literally)
Going overboard (metaphorically)
Poor hospitality
Funding shortages that prevent states from
    doing maintenance work on bridges
Zombie stocks
Has-beens
Nickel-and-diming
Murdered aid workers
Putting economic value on human life
Baby penguins washing up dead onshore
Old money
New money
Electrical fires
People staying alive by eating grass
Government bailouts
Waking up to find people have written all over
    your face in Magic Marker
Coldhearted cads
Flip-floppers
Pitfalls
Pratfalls

Incoherence
Violence in Juarez, Mexico
Corrupt police officers
Shootouts
The death of Doc Holliday
People who define themselves by the labels
    they wear
Rust-colored tap water
Huffing and puffing
Heavy black eyeliner
Claustrophobia
Chandra Levy
Six-year-olds in beauty pageants
Frantic phone calls
Photographs of you passed out in your own
    vomit
Caning
The fact that portable electronic devices allow
    the government to precisely track our
    whereabouts
Immaturity
Crimes against humanity
Oscar winners who forget to thank their
    husbands or wives
Saber rattling
Intertribal warfare
Rocket-propelled bombs
Hollywood marriages broken up by affairs
    with costars
Drama queens

Bank failures
CDs skipping
The Pain Ray, which uses microwave radiation
    to produce burning sensations in victims
Fantasy lives
Folk remedies that don't work
Lechery
Being in debt to the company store
People who talk about yoga all the time
Swallowing your yawns
Pastel suits
Overteased hair
Dogs humping your leg
The smell of the East River
New Age philosophy
Cold fried chicken
President Omar al-Bashir of Sudan
Vague language
Fraudulent Medicare claims
Failing to meet targets for reducing
    greenhouse gas emissions
The Taliban's disavowal of any knowledge of
    attacks that kill large numbers of civilians
Bombings at embassies
Unfulfilled campaign promises
"The Monkey's Paw"
The Grim Reaper
Children with ear infections
Horse tranquilizers
Dying of the hiccups

Mobsters who are forced to put their feet in
  buckets of concrete before being shot
Spitballs
Thunderheads
Water cyclones
Chattering teeth
Trees falling on houses
Covert government installations
Necrologists
Bullfighting
Losing weight in all the wrong places
Gaining weight in all the wrong places
Pulling weeds
Skiing into a tree
Enormous purses
Dial tones
Instant pudding
The Bataan Death March
Taxation without representation
Materialism
Calls from collection agencies
Leaving your car windows open when it's
  raining
The interest rates on credit cards
Falling asset prices
Spurting arteries
Hard questions
Hard answers
Mercenaries
The jet set

Fetid dreadlocks
Workers on assembly lines
Valium
Misdemeanors
Track marks
Drug kingpins
Reckless driving
Fatalism
Single parents
Psychobabble
Phenobarbitol
Tight waistbands
Low thread counts
Judgment Day
Having a job
Not having a job
Childproof packaging
Canned meat
Pyromaniacs
Seaweed in the ocean
Broken umbrellas
File cabinets
Shoes that don't fit right
Having to wear a tie
Rush Limbaugh
Slipping on a banana peel
Stolen bicycles
Subdivisions
Rocky beaches
Jeans that don't button anymore

Step siblings
Censorship
Sagging mattresses
Sagging skin
Ingrown hairs
Bad grammar
Nonrenewable resources
The destitute
Your body mass index
Enlarged pores
Street urchins
Rubber vomit
Getting sand in your bathing suit
Cold soup
Birthdays
Cupcakes
Tchotchkes
High-rises
Mall parking lots
Immortal night
Vinyl siding
Vinyl pants
Noxious fumes
Bad grades
Flowered wallpaper
Nautical themes
Clowns
Overflowing trash cans
The post office the day before Mother's Day
Cement

Stubble

Ringworm
Graffiti
Dropping the soap
Dropping the soap in prison
Your tent collapsing
Lint
Leaky air mattresses
Leaky boats
Unraveling sweaters
Houseguests
Surprise parties
Bobblehead dolls
Tangled Christmas lights
Tangled webs
Icy sidewalks
Heredity
Dents
Piglets nursed by women
Bologna
People who swear around small children
Beer commercials that show debaucherous
    images followed by the words "drink
    responsibly"
Bleach stains
Big shots
Tentacles
Death grips
Manholes
Ragged breathing
Clogged exhaust vents

Practical jokes
Shysters
Stridency
Gag orders
Acrimonious discussions
Cars that talk
Being single at a wedding
Sugar in the salt shaker
Falsely labeled "organic" foods
Field trips from which your child never returns
Exploding diapers
Menus in an unreadable font
Children who are missing key immunizations
Food that's hotter than you anticipated
Chewing ice cubes
Failed attempts to kill your pet
Failed attempts to kill your husband
American bistros and cafés that try to be
    European
Child molesters in pools
Overly protective fathers
Being tied to a rock and thrown into a lake
Accidentally killing your mom
Killing your mom on purpose
Sorceresses who turn men into swine
Children exposed to radon
Blues singers with correct grammar
Real estate scams
Rooms in which each wall is a different color
When your doctor is dying

Horrific trampoline accidents
Tinsel
Obnoxious children in romantic restaurants
The chain falling off your bike
Dogs with trust funds
Graphic doodles in notebooks
Pictures of kissing celebrities
Quadruple chins
Men in lingerie
Barbeque fatalities
Eating Jell-O with a straw
Mistaking dog food for cereal
Fatal skiing accidents
Sex tips from your teenager
Christmas trees that catch fire
People who speak loudly to foreigners
The bottom line
Athletes turned actors
Athletes turned rapists
Disappointing garage sale revenues
Alliterative gas station names
Failed fabulists
Street food in Mexico City
Shingles
Lightning storms while hiking on mountains
Gentle names for horrific hurricanes
People who harmonize outside of college a
    cappella concerts
Meals that take weeks to digest
Wellness

Bankers who call themselves "quants"

Chain-smoking middle schoolers

Clothes designed by rappers

Having a muscular man's cigarette
extinguished on your neck

Verbally abused caddies

Physically abused caddies

Being transferred to Tulsa

Inappropriate obsessions with tofu

Exported holidays

Satan's minions

Children named adverbs

Companies that boast about their corporate
culture

Being kidnapped and subsequently beheaded

Flow charts

Brush fires

Earls fallen from royal favor

Living in the garage

Acronyms whose meaning has been forgotten

Astroturf lawns

People who create their own shade

Being on a bad youth soccer team

Girls named Michael

Wife swapping

Nocturnal emissions

Witches that sink

Children whose role models are cartoon
animals

Urine-stained bathroom floors

Layovers on red-eye flights

Fat men who aren't jolly

Compulsive hair touching

Overhearing your parents discussing how
disappointing you are

Legion forces of darkness

Self-described "ass men"

Forgetful pharmacists

Garish wallpaper

Breaking in new shoes

Defiled church clothes

Models' pouts

Similes involving clouds

Commercials for things that can kill you

Blood sloshing in boots

Broken fire escapes

Dressing your husband

Mixing up your grandchildren's names

Droughts during harvest

Evacuated bowels

Children visiting their incarcerated parents

The vertically challenged

The phrase "vertically challenged"

Graffiti on flawless stone statues

Hunting near hiking trails

Breached city walls

Men without necks

The phrase "You go, girl!"

Hitler trivia

Cereal boxes with stories on them

Coughing to avoid conversation
Dog models
Hitchhiking fugitives
Sentence-long chapters
People who cry during the national anthem
Toddlers addressed as "master" by their
    servants
Forgotten pogroms
Unsuccessful urban rejuvenation projects
Confusing repression with restraint
Hit-and-runs with shopping carts
Being kicked by someone wearing cleats
Little boys who say "yo"
Anecdotes ruined by poor comic timing
Arcane garbage removal laws
Tans that later kill you
Kids who are smaller than their backpacks
Minor characters in lesser novels
Work personas
Mexican restaurant names involving "loco"
Waiters who call themselves servers
Mandatory corporate nametags
Laws against sodomy
Dying of heat
Stepping on crippled birds
Extinct gods
Being unable to afford the funeral
Chronic pain that eludes diagnosis
Chopping off your pinky
Kids who cry when they're tickled

Uninformative suicide notes
Old women who leave their money to their dog
Paying for bottled tap water
Overuse of the prefix "meta"
Burning mouth syndrome
People whose lives are cautionary tales
Al Capone's taxes
Hidden fees
Naked babies in public
Pretentious comedies about bourgeois
    dysfunction
Children who have discovered sarcasm
The archived shopping lists of dead geniuses
Irrelevant displays of erudition
Organic dog food
Toddlers run over by semis
Waking up next to your grandmother
Illegally parked cop cars
White people speaking to their servants in
    bad Spanish
People who do impressions
Negligent crossing guards
Broken generators
Failed transplants
Losing count
Captivity
Loud barrel-chested men
Boys with beards
Blow jobs obtained through bribery
Operating on your child

Being taken up on your impulsive offer to be a
    surrogate mother
Graft
Being left on the side of the road
Muttering in dismay
Dogs drowned in bathtubs
Wicked animals in Disney movies
$10,000 watches
Overlooking function for form
Overlooking form for function
Children crying for their mothers
Mad glee
Cold comfort
Sweetbreads
Blowtorch accidents
Overhyped movies that aren't as good as
    everyone says
Waiting to be rescued
December skies
Phantoms
Eyeglass chains
Noises made by large animals
Creatures in Bosch paintings
Snail trails
The color of burned flesh
The laughter of the damned
Being asked when you're planning to do
    something real with your life
Soldiers cutting off their enemies' ears as
    souvenirs

Embroidered samplers
Nazi war criminals hiding in South America
Primordial ooze
Carnage
Losing an earring
Losing an earring back
The seven vials
Freckles
Sunburned shoulders
Stained butcher's aprons
Wetting the bed
Spooky attics
Falling down a well
Misusing nautical terminology
Monster waves
Scaring your children
The bratty kids of shipping magnates
Too much mayonnaise
Bleeding breasts
Urology
Dogs that are trained to use the toilet
Excessive eyebrow motion
Preschool teachers given to weeping
Rags-to-riches stories
Riches-to-rags stories
TV shows referred to as "cultural events"
Bathroom doors that don't lock
Learning that your lover is fourteen
Dying of the common cold
Being mistaken for a prostitute

Families with incomes larger than the GDP of
    small nations
The Spanish Civil War
Being mistaken for your father
Stupid jobs with huge salaries
Color-coded threat levels at airports
Pets that aren't housebroken
Cultivating a mysterious persona
Emotion in excess of its occasion
Pompous elder statesmen
Missing persons who are actually dead
Aging disgracefully
Centipedes
Fans crushed to death at book signings
Noisy libraries
Cracked, bleeding lips
Explosions in crowded marketplaces
Minor senators with bodyguards
Assistant proofreaders at financial newspapers
Horrible translations of great books
The economy of Zimbabwe
Teachers hoarse from screaming
Moody seventeen-year-olds reading Sylvia Plath
Elderly women who aren't offered a seat
Failed attempts to glamorize novelists
Being shushed by strangers
Gangsters who are role models
College students who think giving their dogs
    beer is funny
Night shift at the morgue

Landscape paintings in diners
Getting an epidural
Shopping as self-expression
Butterflies pinned to classification cards
Hierarchical friendships
Guns with broken safeties
Losing at Russian roulette
Neon colored contacts
Degrees in haircutting
The thighs of nuns
Glowing red rodent eyes
Snarkiness
Accidental strangulation on rope swings
Surprise inspections
Ticks removed with matches
Lost cameras with irreplaceable photos on them
Having more servants than family members
Clubbing (in night clubs)
Clubbing (hitting people with clubs)
Nude beaches
Knowing the words for genitals in many
    languages
Children with stock portfolios
Glabrous bosoms
Ominous men in straw fedoras
Thighs that extend below the knees
Political speeches about courage
Men who refuse to wear condoms
Writers who give interviews about their
    "creative process"

Professional Scrabble players
Rich people who boast of humble origins
Cryptic plots meant to be profound
Therapy sessions in public places
The idea that the self can be perfected
    through reason
Cover charges
People who are exempt from cover charges
Dying on graduation day
Religious people who get extra days off work
Strenuous cleverness
Turning into your mother
Impounded vehicles
Visible armpit hair
Twinkies for dinner
The emperor of ice cream
Getting the boot
Maintenance workers run over by trains
Watching senior citizens make out
The male midriff
People who believe commercials
Telling the same stories over and over
Children who fall into toilets
Panic buttons
Flimsy bike helmets
Men with emotions
Men without emotions
Being your own best friend
Bonuses spent on health care
Nostalgic children

Genius that strikes when you don't have a pen
The insanity defense
What lies beneath
Politicking
People whose lives don't reflect their beliefs
Vitriolic breakup letters
Four-day bus rides
Babysitters who call babies "clients"
The Swiss avant-garde
Once-good actors in soup commercials
Collapsed tunnels
Piglets nursed by women
Babies named after Vikings
Seeing up your teacher's dress
Wardrobe malfunctions
Not knowing why the caged bird sings
Breast-feeding in moving vehicles
People who quote poems by Hallmark
Lightning storms at electrical plants
Former presidents who get to cut in line
Profanity-laced yelling matches
Not wanting to have sex with your wife
Men who call female dogs bitches
Men who call women bitches
Stale donuts for dinner
All-girls schools
Baking on hot days
Never quite mastering a second language
Having sex with someone you don't respect
Failed drug tests

People who say nice things in mean tones of
   voice
People who say mean things in nice tones of
   voice
Splitting hairs
Splitting atoms
Untamed shrews
Falling asleep at your child's wedding
Being dead in the water
Married men masturbating
Renaissance men
Baby names chosen by committee
Boring parties without alcohol
Boring parties with alcohol
Great-grandmothers in tank tops
Having a conversation with the back of
   someone's head
Ellis Island
Dogs without necks
Not knowing how to proceed
Being called on when you don't know the
   answer
Bad music while you're on hold
Uncontrollable sweating
Wild beasts in flimsy cages
Getting lost while jogging
Incompetent projectionists
Saving a seat in a crowded movie theater for
   someone who never shows up
Running out of Zoloft at a family reunion

Fat men in rickshaws
Drunken toasts at weddings that reveal how
    many sexual partners the groom has had
People who believe they are the Messiah
Children on leashes
Children with muzzles
Preteen girls who shave their legs
Ricin—one of the deadliest poisons known to —
    man
Stupid people who went to Yale
Carrying heavy grocery bags long distances
News stories that equate protestors with
    terrorists
Humans fed through stump grinding machines
Being crushed by a massive boulder
The shortest person in the world
Insecurities that ruin relationships
Regional branch managers
Lightning at the pool
Never being found during hide and seek
Comparing your beloved to a camel
Vectors of transmission
Meaningless adjectives
Tall ladders in strong winds
What's considered newsworthy
Waking up early on Saturday even though the
    alarm wasn't set
The fate of worms after rain
Parents who furtively read their
    children's diaries

Kids sent to boarding school against
  their wishes
Attribution errors
Disliking the other people on the chain gang
Killer tomatoes
People who use the word "communist" as an
  insult
Longing for dawn
Vituperation
Spikenards
Relapsed junkies
Sleeping sentries
Dating a girl you can't lift
Public toilets in Egypt
Meaningless adjectives
Tall ladders in strong winds
What's considered newsworthy
Pits of poisonous snakes
Children who fall into old unmarked mineshafts
Startling a grizzly bear
Honorifics
The minions of the rich
Stabbing yourself on a knife while doing
  dishes in a soapy sink
Children used as minefield sweepers
Comic actors trying to do serious drama
Graduating from high school at age forty
Pesticides that kill the family dog
Children voted least likely to succeed
Weak points

Evil twins

Inordinate excitement caused by celebrity
 sightings
Silver medalists
Economic policies that exacerbate financial
 downturns
Children who idolize Napoleon
The higher incidence of diabetes among lower
 income people
Parents who track their children via GPS
The smell of stale vomit
Restless leg syndrome
Trains that are not in service
Bypassed subway stops
Children who experience withdrawal
 symptoms without TV
Euphemisms for death
Crowded buses on hot days
Shared lovers
Shared napkins
Shared bathrooms
Recreational knife sharpening
Down syndrome
Self-cut hair
Shaving cuts that require stitches
Pointed throat clearing
Acting on passing impulses
The death of your horse
Broken roller coasters
Confusing directions
Fingers cut off by fans

Cities in which the quality of municipal services
     depends on the race of the neighborhood
Sexually active tweens
High-functioning alcoholics
Doing an internship at the local insane asylum
Having to sell the cow
Buttons with slogans about saving the world
News programs that show close-ups of
     weeping mourners on a daily basis
Fistfights between fathers and sons
Cubicle workers longing for transcendent
     experiences in nature
Alienating architecture of the postwar period
Fatal overconfidence
Things that remind you of dead people
Slugs having sex
Diamond-studded flip-flops
Professional matchmakers
Centers for vaginal surgery
Soldiers on antidepressants
The real estate value of houses where people
     were brutally murdered
Knee-high socks with shorts
Angry chimpanzees
Transparent marketing ploys
Twaddle
Old women who address all young men
     as "lover"
Boxers with torn retinas
Fantasies about killing your boss' children

Cures discovered after a disease has killed a
　　member of your family
Warlords with sensitive sides
The book selection at provincial libraries
Holding yourself to a lower standard than
　　everyone else
Holding yourself to a higher standard than
　　everyone else
Overcrowded restaurants at brunch
Dissertations about sitcoms
People with the same first and last name
Becoming homosexual to get attention
Art based on despair
Clichéd epiphanies
Impoverished balloon artists
Anchormen pretending to care about the
　　people killed in the latest earthquake
People wealthy enough to postpone their death
Skinny people who complain that they're fat
Fat people who complain that they're skinny
Soggy strawberries
People whose death is funny
Dogs killed with pitchforks
Parents who skip their kids' softball games
Captives clutching the bars of their cages
Feeling dirty afterward
Dogs barking at the wind
Playas who drive Nissans
Half-dead mice struggling in traps
Arcane Eastern methods of torture

Fallen saints
Scholarly feuds
Deadly tornadoes that kill Boy Scouts
African jackals gnawing corpses
Abandoned conversations
Photographs ruined by rain
Bloodstained stones
Treacherous generals
Cankers of the conscience
Unheeded prophets
The inhabitants of Dante's lowest circle of Hell
Conferences at which academics discuss
    homelessness
People who use "brunch" as a verb
Children who want to be lawyers when they
    grow up
Getting the runaround
The sex lives of early Puritans
Dropped calls
Neverland Ranch
The fact that 45 percent of people ages eighty-
    five and over have Alzheimer's disease
Poodles mauled by raccoons
Housewives who want to die
Nontortured artists
Backfiring cars that induce panic in Vietnam
    veterans
Soldiers of fortune
Pornographic violence
Sex scenes with aging actors

Burglars who sue the people they robbed for
    getting injured during a robbery
Mace in the eyes
Stomach wounds
Sloths
Tone-deaf people who sing along to recordings
Funhouse mirrors
Aging porn stars
Ichthyosis vulgaris—a disorder that causes
    dry, scaly skin
Dick Cheney shooting his friends
The presidency of Grover Cleveland
Distressed clothing
Diasporas
Repetitive operas in Sanskrit
Purses that are more valuable than their
    contents
Guys who are too old to be in the club
Nostalgic expatriates
Pretentious poems about trembling leaves in
    autumn
William Wallace
The fact that some suicide bombers believe
    they will be greeted by forty virgins
People who drop out of school to play video
    games
Choosing death over dishonor
Choosing dishonor over death
Rainy weekends
Fetuses tossed in dumpsters

Campaigns to stop kids from killing homeless
people
Fetal alcohol syndrome
Taking orders from people who are dumber
than you
Whales killed by golf balls in their blowholes
Presidents judged by their sexual habits
Gossip about celebrities that is intentionally
leaked
The death of John Belushi
Attractive girls who flirt their way out of
speeding tickets
People who argue by repeating the same
phrase over and over
The taste of Red Bull
The death of Tchaikovsky
Smoking through a stoma (a hole in the neck)
People who find desecration erotic
Drinking expired milk and becoming
violently ill
Children of therapists who have disastrous
mental problems
People who always ask black people if they
like basketball
People who think Beethoven was a painter
Cracking under pressure
Poltroons
People who take the weather personally
Performers with crippling stage fright
Painfully beautiful songs

Painfully unbeautiful songs

Drowning in the shallow end

Burning crosses

People who think aloud

The shadow of the moon

Tenors with nasal voices

Dreaming of things you don't have

Living below a flamenco dancer

Horny people with latex allergies

Women who pretend they have thyroid
    problems

International business trips for a single meeting

Cows awaiting slaughter

Parents who are ashamed of their
    daughter's pregnancy

Adoptive parents who return their children

Being rejected by an egg donor agency

Learning about your father from a
    Google search

Still having a babysitter at age fifteen

Failing to advance to the next level of
    amateur ballet

Gymnastics fatalities

Failing out of bartending school

The faint smell of feces in nursing homes

Becoming immune to caffeine

Three-legged puppies

Snobs at the opera

U.S. presidents that get stuck in the bathtub
    (William Howard Taft)

Undistinguished drag queens
The only fat kid in a dance recital
Being unable to break a board at karate class
Failing to win your sweetheart a stuffed bear
    at the carnival
Being asked to join the carnival
Drowning on dry land
Losing the Olympic gold medal for your team
Pairs of ragged claws scuttling across the
    floors of silent seas
Powdered hot chocolate in a Styrofoam cup
Vegans in cattle country
Moldy cheesecake
People who go to war to have some good stories
Love affairs squashed by disapproving parents
Children whose morals are derived from
    cartoons
Preparing a meal for your child's imaginary
    friend
Laid-off single mothers with young children
Movie projectors that break at climactic
    moments
Bad seafood in landlocked states
Failed voodoo
Lord Byron's pillow, which was filled with the
    pubic hair of his lovers
Teenage poetry about suicide
People who die during sex
Celebrity look-alikes
Retirees in Florida waiting to die

The smoking section of restaurants
Failed attempts to join the mile high club
Existential crises after the age of twenty-eight
Graphing the slope of your stomach
Corporate suppression of humor
Gratuitous e-mail forwards
Swallowing too much chlorine
Irregularly inspected Ferris wheels
Overweight people at amusement parks
Confusing your birth control pills with aspirin
Confusing aspirin with your birth control pills
Forced religious conversions
Being ten cents short at the toll booth
Confiding in a bartender
Denying thy father and refusing thy name
"This quintessence of dust"
Aborted plans to abandon your family
Secrets that aren't secret
Braces that make your teeth worse
Mute roosters
Debates about unanswerable questions
Great job offers in godforsaken places
People who can only listen to music with lyrics
Talentless monkeys
Poems that rhyme "create" with "defecate"
Elderly people who compare themselves to
    aged wine
Meals described as "taste adventures"
Parents who tell their children they look sexy
The omnivore's dilemma

The number of hours in a day

People whose self-worth derives from
    victories in board games

Kids who always complain about being bored

Postal workers reading your mail

People who make millions because of their
    personality

Obscure senators from Nebraska

Government subsidies to the corn industry

Industrialized food

The treatment of the animals in your dinner

Choking on pubic hair

Countries in which women are property

Small farmers forced to sell their land

Body parts caught in escalators

Spotted dick (the food)

Spotted dick

Falling corn prices

Cows fed the remains of cows

Reluctant grooms

Deriving joy from food that increases your
    risk of death

Pretentious buildings in America named for
    things in England

Appeasing genocidal dictators

Kings who deflower and murder the local
    maidens

Trying to schedule a plumber

Half-assed vows of undying love

Being chained by the neck to a tree

Maiden voyages that are also last voyages
The disproportionate incarceration rate of
    black men
Actuarial tables
Couples who look bad together
White people who wear blackface for Halloween
Veterans who are ashamed of their service
Fear of wearing bathing suits
Cathedrals turned banks
Stalled initiatives
Swindlers
Needing a degree to tend bar
Burying a horse
Horizontal learning curves
The limits of Freudian analysts
Gradually failing restaurants that give their
    owners ulcers
Angry hogs
Attributing moral qualities to food products
The baffling profusion of new technologies
People with bad credit who get loans
People with good credit who are denied loans
Debates between stupid people
Trying to eat while driving
Getting fired on your first day of work
Being unable to answer your child's simple
    questions
For-profit non-profits
Manure lagoons
Dying of laughter

Bad foster parents
Prisoners who try to commit suicide by
    swallowing toothpaste
Nuclear winter
Not knowing what the ingredients in a
    product mean
Broken handles on heavy suitcases
Diaphragms that get stuck
Cows that sleep in their own shit
Feeling inferior to your children
Getting caught having sex in a movie theater
Going to an overpriced restaurant with people
    you dislike
Documentaries about bricks
Inadvertently helping your enemy
Medication that causes continuous drooling
Learning that your ex-lover's new lover is
    better in bed than you
Impoverished lords forced to dust their own
    castles
Children who fall down laundry chutes
Hating your job but having nothing else to
    talk about
Homeless men eating garbage
Choosing starvation over cannibalism
Choosing cannibalism over starvation
Losing in double overtime
Lack of hand-eye coordination
Death and dismemberment
Photographs of places you'll never go

Corrupt Roman tour guides

Rent

Working as a mascot at Disney World

Factories of death

Eating raw chicken hearts

Casus belli

Inside jobs

Being unable to visit your grandmother due to
immigration laws

Williamsburg

Corn-fed cows

Hand-me-down underwear

Secret CIA prisons

Disneyland Resort Paris

Getting fired before you can quit

Museums of technology

Stale bagels

Awkward encounters with your therapist at
the grocery store

Losing both of your parents in the same year

The crumbling of the Ottoman Empire

People who answer rhetorical questions with
yes or no

Progress

Being stabbed with a pen

Sameness

Learning your beloved is married

Golf

Ancient Greek grammar

People who want to measure Einstein's brain

Microtonal wailing

Relatives who ask you to borrow large sums of money

Smashing your laptop in a fit of rage

People who consider Sudoku intellectual

Trendy self-laceration

Walking corpses

Bad language poets

Gay men whose fathers despise them

Nincompoops

Expensive used books

J. Robert Oppenheimer, the father of the atomic bomb

Superfans

Not getting to say good-bye to a dying relative because of flight delays

The Axis powers

Grade inflation

White men singing the blues

The sleeping habits of parents of newborns

Babies on life support

Lying about the race of your adopted child

Permanent chickenpox scars

Having to tip five different porters in the same hotel

Coming home to find the locks changed

Leaving the refrigerator door open overnight

Poor Republicans

Wealthy Democrats

Destination weddings you can't afford to attend

Lisa Novak, the astronaut who drove five
hundred miles wearing diapers to try to
kidnap her romantic rival
Vomiting during a presentation
Being overheard laughing at someone who
fell over
Rap music in foreign languages
Ten-year-olds who worry about college
admissions
Digressions within digressions
Kierkegaard
Self-pity while washing the dishes
Sudden epiphanies about the eternal oblivion
that awaits us all
Dessert withdrawal symptoms
Baby's first swear word
The thirty-eight ingredients in a Chicken
McNugget
Businessmen talking about their boring lives
on trains
Malfunctioning garbage disposals
Cleaning out the kitchen drain with your
bare hand
Losing pressure
Accidents on oil rigs
Cornholing
Not having enough time to read
White rappers
Pictures of celebrities buying groceries
Dying while rock climbing

Dogs as fashion accessories
Being boiled alive
Cowboy boots north of the Mason-Dixon Line
Never striking gold
Manually unclogging the toilet
Children with a different tutor for every subject
Forty-year-old men in boy bands
Black lipstick
Self-appointed fashion police
Idolizing idiots
Rheumatism
Military officials at Guantanamo Bay using the
    show *24* as inspiration for torture tactics
Atrophied instincts
Being booed off stage
Electric blankets that short circuit and roast
    you alive
Bad imitations of Henry James
People who say intelligent things by accident
Cats on IV drips
Drowned lifeguards
Flammable carcinogens in fast food
Antidepressants that kill your sex drive
Entire albums about a single breakup
Classical music sampled in hip-hop songs
Not realizing that the smallest details of your
    life are part of a vast geopolitical chain of
    death and oppression
Potato chips as an aperitif
Corporate field trips

The stench of strangers' sweat
Renting a designer handbag
Oprah
Parents who spend thousands of dollars
    framing their children's preschool artwork
College courses about reality television
Leopard skin carpeting
Men who treat their girlfriends like their
    mothers
Men who treat their mothers like their
    girlfriends
Seven-year-olds in strollers
Environmentalists chained to the tops of tall
    trees that are cut down
People with multiple iPods to match different
    outfits
Involuntary racist thoughts
Human troughs
Being unable to afford the ambulance bill
The hypoxic zone in the Gulf of Mexico
Agricultural monocultures
Food-like edible substances
Dying during driving school
Funding with strings attached
Lipophobia
Summer colds caused by air conditioning
Rivers of chicken blood flowing across
    factory floors
People who write in library books
Taking sled jumps on a wooden toboggan

Rats allowed to eat themselves to death in the
interest of science
Chain reactions that destroy fragile ecosystems
Eating urban tree fruit
Babies forgotten on trains
Accident-prone individuals
Deadly wild berries
Fungiphobia
Dying in an ambulance
Books that should have ended hundreds of
pages ago
People who get mean when they're hungry
Mistaking kilometers for miles on the speed
limit sign
Celebrities whose felonies only enhance their
mystique
Torpedoed sailboats
The last time you have sex before you die
UFDA regulations that discourage local
farming and agriculture
Having to move in one day
Orthorexia—an obsession with eating only
healthy food
Regional cuisines eliminated by globalization
Horace Fletcher, aka the Great Masticator,
who introduced the practice of chewing
each bite one hundred times
Hourly enemas
The Cartesian belief that animals lack a soul
and thus don't feel pain

Proselytizing vegans
Leaving lewd voice mails on your lover's
	family phone
Profuse sweating on first dates
Metaphors comparing acne to volcanoes
Human fans
Stress that causes hemorrhoids
Being your own mover
Dyed facial hair
Adults who just want to be held
The smell of strange men's feet
Missing persons
Bedtime
Purely financial motivations
Pregnant women who get punched in the
	stomach
Not being invited to the funeral
Parents who deny their kids nothing
Parents who deny their kids everything
Standing around waiting to be spoken to
Alfred Nobel, founder of the Nobel Peace
	Prize, inventor of dynamite
Bosses who stand around watching everyone
	else work
Chalk outlines
Finishing the day with one less finger than
	you started with
Waking up the baby by having sex
Old men's thighs
Losing your virginity in a moving vehicle

The contradiction at the heart of the world
  (Nietzsche)
Endangered languages
Decapitated street dogs
The persistence of trivial memories
Intractable knots of anxiety
Chinese couples who sell bootleg videos on
  blankets
Full-speed collisions of outfielders
The correlation between education level and
  age at marriage
Swaziland, which has the lowest life
  expectancy in the world (32.2 years)
Dogs licking their own testicles
Making sheepish apologies for the drunken
  blunders of friends
Treating the homeless with condescension
Shampoo that makes your hair fall out
Losing your child to a cult
The sound of a bomb falling from the sky
Neighborhoods in which you feel invisible
Rich people remodeling their already
  gorgeous homes
People who see minorities in a restaurant and
  assume that they are waiters
Your wife discovering your porn collection
Men in bikinis
Falling asleep while receiving oral sex
Falling asleep while giving oral sex
Bright sterilized smiles

The smell of hand sanitizer

Musicals about drug addicts

The sudden urge to kill a baby

Unrealistic movies about divorced couples who stay friends and love their kids even more than before

The runner of the first marathon, who dropped dead afterward

Turkish soldiers who used the Parthenon to store gunpowder

Books that make you stupider

Stupid actors playing intelligent characters

Making your mother worry

Fires preceded by the word great

Learning that your daughter was defiled and deflowered

Concrete blast walls

Blood drives that don't collect much blood

The American culture of debt

David Addington, chief architect of the legal strategy for the war on terror

Manacles

Prisoners who are forced to defecate on themselves

Chinese supermarkets with entire aisles devoted to MSG

The man behind the curtain

Wage stagnation

Studies showing that most women who get breast cancer don't have a family history

Women dropping out of the work force
Home-schooled kids with no social skills
The death of Narcissus
Pains in phantom limbs
Studies that indicate that most people think
    they're more attractive than they really are
Evil henchmen
Girls gone wild
Fare hikes
Having to tighten your belt
Having to loosen your belt
Budgeting errors that make deficits look like
    surpluses
The smell of fish markets
Disodium phosphate
Believing frozen yogurt is good for you
Studies showing that 3 percent of teenage
    girls have been victims of dating violence
Drinking games that turn deadly
Unused gym memberships
Failed attempts to flee your origins
The golden light of car commercials
Conversation as performance
Filibusters
The diameter of Toni Morrison's thighs
Drug-related kidnappings in Colombia
Accidentally revealing your true feelings
Indiscriminate praise
Rabid sports fans
Men who slap strange women on the ass

Chronically late people
Depressed narrators in Graham Greene novels
People who like themselves
Insanely competitive soccer parents
Flirtatious love bites that draw blood
Road head that leads to fiery death
Ambiguous idiomatic sayings
Abandoned industrial cores
People who can't point to their kidneys
Artificial sweeteners that cause cancer
Infants possessed by Satan
Economies of scale
Curdled milk
Trendy metaphysics
Mattress professionals
Man breasts
Jeans in August
Ribald macho ribbing
Overly clever Nabokov novels
Not knowing how to pronounce Nabokov
People who are beyond reproach
Male bonding through misogyny
Falling through the cracks
The apparent agelessness of Demi Moore
People with no conversational finesse
Anonymous urban living
The disappearance of pay phones
Men who live in bus stations
State-controlled media monopolies
The distant sound of approaching warriors

Requiems
for dreams

Being traded for a mule

The anatomy of melancholy

Jiggling fat deposits

Overhearing your husband talking to his
mistress

Self-promoting student council members

Fetishes involving mustard

Irrational arguments

Sinecures

Botched aphorisms

Cell phone worship

Studies showing that the U.S. leads the world
in rates of experimenting with marijuana
and cocaine

Bathroom attendants

Summary judgments

Tattoos acquired while drunk

Hedonists

Perpetual drizzle

Irrational hatred of strangers

Puzzling instruction manuals

Indiscreet belching

Aging commuters

Your daughter's boyfriend

Deities who rape mortals

Schadenfreude

State-sponsored murder

Paper shuffling jobs

Weeks without sunlight

The deaths of cultural icons

Excel spreadsheets
Inscrutable motives
Authors on the lecture circuit
White bread
Sexualized firemen
Terse, stolid men
Moby-Dick
Tomorrow
Yesterday
Forty-year-old actors who are still "aspiring"
The slings and arrows of outrageous fortune
Agitprop
Inanely repetitive techno music
The second law of thermodynamics
The fading beauty of the vain
Smerdyakov
Not living well
Not loving much
Not laughing often
The decline of letter writing
Forgotten genocides
Vividly remembered genocides
The Manhattan Project
Grueling tests of endurance
Developmental disabilities
The problems of the rich
Food that resembles feces
Misguided energy
Mixed metaphors
Verbal lashings

Horse whipping (of horses)
Horse whipping (of people)
Token minorities
The docility of the oppressed
Novelists corrupted by fame
Pointless innovation
Crocodile-infested rivers
Death masks
Black sheep
Forgotten folk melodies
Napalmed villages
Agent Orange
Power-hungry cops
Army recruiters
Soot-blackened faces
Schizophrenics on public transportation
Brand names that become nouns
Being exhorted to feel civic pride
People with a great capacity for silent suffering
Dogs that serve as surrogate children
Children that serve as surrogate dogs
Incredibly healthy people
Minor bureaucrats
Tetrasodium polyphosphate
Fingers slammed in doors
Paternity tests
Longing for a preindustrial past
Parents who steal from their children's
    piggy banks
Paranoia about suitcases in airports

Elderly people and stairs
Prolific mediocre poets
Irrelevant digressions
Simplistic reasoning
Not remembering a language you once knew
The silent machinations of your enemies
Exchanges of banalities
Competitive eating
Bad teachers who ruin great books
Little boys who are obsessed with obscure
        weapons
Knowing how uninteresting your thoughts are
Despoiled mountain parks
Being forgotten by posterity
Being remembered wrongly by posterity
Songs about fucking bitches and shooting
        people
Neglected filial responsibilities
Constant self-censorship
Lingering deaths
The siege of Sarajevo
Having shit for brains
Midnight gluttony
Crippled veterans of senseless wars
Racist anthropologists
Starving people
Well-fed dogs
Zero-sum games
Subspecialties
Exotic game hunting

Deposed monarchs
Mustard breath
Exercise motivated by self-hatred
Small errors with big consequences
The dispossessed
Beautiful married people
Civilized barbarities
Cheerful answering machines
People with the power to ruin your life
Intimate confessions to strangers
Jocular racism
The sound of saws cutting through metal
Obsolete technologies
Cunning little vixens
The human lifespan
Perennial bestsellers
Watching TV to avoid conversation
Sangfroid
Polysorbate 80
Biographies of minor TV actors
Sentence fragments
Watery gruel
Trendy Eastern philosophies
Tambourine players
Piles of skinned hogs
Lecherous backpackers in youth hostels
The percentage of Americans who vote
The rape of the Sabine women
Wishing you were British
Fallibility

Faded hieroglyphs of doom
Rebellion through promiscuity
Ubiquitous corporate logos
Vast fortunes obtained through obscure means
Impoverished Russian widows
Sunsets made beautiful by air pollution
Exhausted ingenuity
Exhortations to "be yourself"
Politics as a blood sport
Hospital waiting rooms
Sex as conquest
Toilet paper commercials
Sewage treatment centers
Trying to talk to your extended family
Failed efforts at reform
Early flying machines
Headless statues of angels
Knowing smiles
The sexualization of cars
Crack babies
Becoming the thing you hate most
People who talk to their televisions
Preachers who mispronounce the groom's
    name
Bloody revolts in distant lands
Pretentious neologisms
Cultural variation in standards of hygiene
Muttered curses
Bidets
Abortive attempts at anal sex

Endless journeys
Fake bonhomie
Men nicknamed "Ducky"
Getting sawdust in your eyes
Invaders from the North
Electra
Electra complexes
Children growing up
Children not growing up
The overuse of irony
Memoirs disguised as fiction
Fiction disguised as memoir
The illusion that science is infallible
Minor strokes
Mono- and diglycerides
Radovan Karadzic—former Serbian leader and
    war criminal
Long irrelevant political scandals that deflect
    attention away from the issues
Myalgic encephalomyelitis—a chronic
    inflammatory disease
Lemmings
Piercings done at parties
The lifespan of mayflies
Albinism
Addison's disease
Ballistic missiles
The desire to be liked by your enemies
The fact that Coca-Cola can be used to clean
    highways

Gas stations that charge more when you pay with a credit card

Not being in the VIP section

Putting all your change in a broken parking meter before realizing it's broken

Stray hairs long enough to feel but too short to pluck

Restaurants that don't accept credit cards so they don't have to pay taxes

Using race as the sole basis in deciding to vote for a candidate

Using race as the sole basis to vote against a candidate

Subtle rhetorical attempts to discourage the use of reason

Unsubtle rhetorical attempts to discourage the use of reason

The calculated disclosure of humanizing details

The early years of bitter struggle

Politicians who give irrelevant but charming replies to pointed questions

Itching until you bleed

Teratomas, or tumors with teeth and hair

Perez Hilton

Smegma

The 55 percent of women who report sexual dissatisfaction after a C-section

The 70 percent of women who report sexual dissatisfaction after giving birth vaginally

Smoothies described as "nutrition systems"

White people who address each other as "my nigga"

Emphatic but meaningless toasts

Korsakoff's syndrome—a brain disorder caused by chronic alcoholism

Interviewers who answer their phone just to chat during your job interview

Pretending to have an assistant

Theft from the office fridge

Circumferential burns

Stapled fingers

Memoirs by child molesters

Flip books with missing pictures

Irate retail customers

Hydatiform moles, which make you look pregnant when you're not

Workers who refer to their cubicles as their castles

Playing with your cell phone in an elevator to avoid talking to someone

Hitler's relatives

The fact that the suicide rate is highest among the elderly

Having your house taken by the government and sold to a private corporation

Fake paintings at famous museums

Medicating children with too much candy

Food decaying in gutters

Feminists who oppose abortion

Death by prescription drug overdose

Private detectives who don't lead romantic,
    solitary lives
Nights in the bomb shelter
1508, when Puerto Rican natives decided
    to determine whether Spaniards were
    immortal by holding them underwater
Anarchist parties
Children who think a penny is a fortune
Losing someone else's keys
Late periods
Deceptive descriptions on menus
Beggars who accept money but refuse food
Incidents
The inverse relationship between what you
    contribute to society and your salary
Children who try to leap from one roof to
    another but don't make it
Boyfriends who consider barbeque a romantic
    evening out
Spicy food that causes weeping and
    permanent taste loss
Children playing in Astroturf parks
The telltale heart
Diplomatic immunity
Nations referred to as "them"
Frightening smiles on little girls' dolls
Eating spicy buffalo wings and then rubbing
    your eyes
People who call New York a town
The boy who cried wolf

"Water, water everywhere, and nor any drop to drink"

Air the consistency of soup

Girls who date losers so they can control them

People who think Rambo is a documentary

Not answering when your girlfriend's mom calls

Being too busy for sex

Sight-seeing in Ohio

Taping over your wedding video with porn

Making a porn of your wedding night

Cheek implants

Smelly condensation that develops under the mats in wrestling rooms

Children falling from the backs of pickup trucks

Rising rates of skin cancer among African Americans

Children with more than two daddies

Parents who threaten their kids with foster care

When winning a tournament means you'll be sacrificed to the gods

Surviving a beheading

Roman aqueducts made from lead

The effects of watching childbirth on the male sexual psyche

Cleft lips

Saturnalias ending in death

Cocaine cut with powdered bleach

Drunk clowns at birthday parties

www.cameltoe.com

Toddlers who enjoy death metal

Vegetarians who get salmonella
Children named Salmonella
Mary Jo Kopechne
Eddie Murphy after the eighties
People who pronounce "Mahler" "Mailer"
Munchausen syndrome—a psychiatric
disorder in which people fake disease to
gain sympathy
Munchausen by proxy—in which parents
tell their children that they're sick when
they're not
Tourists who visit the homes of famous
murderers
Gravediggers
Gold diggers
People who bathe in champagne
Grilles (on teeth, not cars)
People who fill vans with speakers and drive
around the block blasting music
Nude actors who get unintentional erections
on stage
Clothed actors who get unintentional
erections on stage
Shouting out "Mom" during sex
Shouting out "Dad" during sex
Shouting out "Grandma" during sex
Shouting out "Grandpa" during sex
Expired bologna
Fat vegans
Road trips to the Mall of America

Groceries forgotten in hot cars

Fanning yourself with a phone book

Blow jobs behind dumpsters

Thrush—a fungal infection

Touching the ass of a strange woman who
looks just like your girlfriend

Suspecting that your infant son is gay

Anorexic women who shop in the juniors
department

Female postmen who just want to be called
postal workers

Somber young men who believe that literature
can change the world

Children's books about the apocalypse

The 6 million British dwellings that lacked
indoor toilets after World War II

Eco-dramas

Nutritional supplements that cause cancer

Towels that smell like cat urine

Stiff, starchy new sheets

Children who think that just saying a bad
word constitutes humor

Wives who pop their husband's pimples

Favorite baseball caps that get too dirty to wear

People who eat only at Burger King

The one in three American children who will
get type 2 diabetes

Questions that are actually statements

Parts of the body that are also known as
cavities

Surgeons who operate on the wrong part of
the body

Not giving a fuck

People who keep their pinky nail long to snort
cocaine

Heavy drinking near cliffs

Children who are constantly told they're perfect

Parties that the host keeps promising will get
better soon

The practice of drinking a mixture of cow's
blood and milk

The sinking of Mexico City

Being paid in salt (from which the word
"salary" derives)

West African tribes that resolve disputes
by poisoning both the accuser and the
accused, believing only the guilty party
will die

The monastery of St. Francis in Portugal,
which has a chapel with human bones
lining its walls and pillars

Trying to high-five someone but missing

Trying to high-five someone but accidentally
slapping them

The dwindling number of traits considered
uniquely human

Unhappily married men who live vicariously
through their sons' sexual exploits

Being asked to fill out forms as your loved one
lies bleeding on the emergency room floor

Waiters who tell you their first names
Desperately clinging to the first topic of
    shared interest in a conversation
Pygmies who love basketball
Terrible restaurants with long waits
All the books that have not yet been translated
    into Braille
People who won't take no for an answer
People who gladly take no for an answer
Not making your fortune until you're too old
    to enjoy it
Coveted internships that consist of sorting
    and stapling papers
Used cell phone salesmen
The unbeautiful
Broken carbon monoxide detectors
Mannequins of ambiguous ethnicity
Gyms that sell junk food
Solitary early morning sessions on the
    treadmill
People who desperately want an excuse to tell
    you where they went to college
Celebrities who endorse snack products that
    would destroy their figures
Asking to be held on a first date
Losing your virginity doggy style
Realizing you have nothing to say to your wife
Sanitary napkins with poor adhesives
Teenagers who spend hours in the bathroom
    doing mysterious things

Giving someone a gift they don't need

Pepenadores—people who make a living scavenging trash dumps in Mexico City

Teachers who justify their cruelty by saying they are preparing students for the real world

Loss of appetite

Loss of interest in formerly pleasurable activities

Attempting to give away once-cherished possessions

Lifelong friends moving away

Belligerent drunks

Periodic heavy sighing

Facile charm

Being exhorted to do the Christian thing when you're not Christian

Passive-aggressive rhetorical questions

Alternating patterns of depression and mania

Bad seeds

Avoidant personality disorder

Stressors

Choosing between the devil and the deep blue sea

Fungi

Raynaud's disease, which causes numbness in certain areas of the body

Cluster headaches

Clusterfucks

The estimated 45 million Americans who suffer chronic or recurring headaches

Emotional inhibition

Gastric secretions

Acid indigestion

Type A personalities

Type B personalities

Studies showing that pessimists tend to have
poorer health

Driving rain

Driving in the rain

Asking God why he has forsaken you

Employees of the month

Running out of wiper fluid

Girls who will talk to you only if you buy them
a drink

Small businesses that are fronts for money
laundering operations

Rapists hiding behind the washing machines
in dorm laundry rooms

Mirages

Gila monsters

Golfball-sized hail

The imprisonment of Geronimo

Trying to find time to get your oil changed

Pilot announcements that begin with "No
need to panic, but . . ."

Washing the family dog

Not washing the family dog

Breaking the cork of a wine bottle

Forgetting to follow the high-altitude cooking
instructions when cooking at high altitude

Penis envy

Castration anxiety

Overcompensating

Spiritual death

The indifference of the universe

Your IQ

Studies showing that over a six month period, 3 percent of men and 7 percent of women developed a depressive disorder

People without handicaps who park in handicapped parking spots

Insulin coma shock

Construction workers on skyscrapers in strong winds

Nosophobia—fear of injury or disease

Hell or high water

Adjustment disorder

Numbness

Somatoform pain disorder

The link between suppressed emotions and cancer

Movies with double-digit box office grosses

Fannie Mae

Freddie Mac

Downward mobility

Catatonia

Tardive dyskinesia—involuntary repetitive movements

The "revolving door effect" at mental hospitals

Affective tolerance

Martha Moxley, who was beaten to death with a golf club by Michael Skakel

Wanting to be sedated

The Alcoholics Anonymous dropout rate of 80 percent

Dexedrine

Methadone clinics

The fact that the American Psychiatric Association considered homosexuality a disorder until 1987

Exhibitionism

Voyeurs

Reaganomics

Demolition of childhood homes

Lost mythologies

Noisily blown noses

Putting your diaphragm in upside down

"Just" wars

Twenty-hour workdays

The demonization of countries

The death of Patroclus

Sinister omens

Riverside squatters

Multi-infarct dementia

Fashionable diseases

The power of context

Bad taste in music

Inveterate gloominess

Crises of faith

The merciless teasing of gentle children

Scurvy

Soft, solitary weeping
Wandering in death's shade
Clattering high heels
Pretentious melancholy
Overmedicated children
Anti-schizophrenia drugs that cause fatal
    blood disorders
Fourteen dollar Portuguese cheese
Disappointing homemade sex videos
People who talk with their mouths full
Televisions in cars
Burned manuscripts
Birds trapped in airports
Men who shave their chests
People who hate people who help them
Drowning in excrement
Monolingual Americans
Folie à deux—in which two people living
    together both develop delusional disorders
Sugar-free ice cream
Meatless meat
Friends without benefits
Your first HIV test
Dyspareunia, or painful sexual intercourse
Selectively enforced laws
Brazilian bikini waxes
Inane corporate mantras
Starbucks
People who remove their shoes in public
Cybersex

People with letters shaved into their scalps
Romeo and Juliet
Invented mental disorders
Miscalculating the height of doors
Forgetting to take your birth control pills
Pressed flowers forgotten between the pages
    of old books
Woody Allen wannabes
Infant clothing boutiques
Pet spas
Power-hungry security guards
Indecipherable health insurance policies
Misdiagnoses
Being the only one at a funeral
Greener grass
Polite applause
Babies without arms
Failures of the imagination
Memory slips
Histrionic personality disorder
Charismatic leaders of doomed cults
Starch
Hyper-rational people
Bricks as murder weapons
Scientific utopias
Corporate efforts to influence media coverage
The romanticization of the irrational
The imprecision of language
Punctured eardrums
The sound of your lover defecating

Abstract expressionism
Effeminate gangsters
Drowning in a vat of chocolate
Circumstantial evidence
Loving someone who doesn't speak your
    language
Being too old to be precocious anymore
Plausible deniability
Exploding parcels
Pranks gone horribly wrong
People who use the word "whippersnapper"
Children who vanish at low tide
Gnawing inner emptiness
Pointlessly inverted syntax
Exophthalmic people, who have abnormally
    bulging eyes
Hubcabs as Christmas ornaments
Sad people who look like frogs
People who don't read fiction because it isn't
    true
Prisons at night
Palpable tension
Herniated discs
Pitbull attacks
Honor among thieves
Pedophiles near playgrounds
De facto slavery
Garish Americana
Self-proclaimed genius
Visible sneeze particles

Realizing that you're boring
Not realizing that you're boring
The ever-growing numbers of bad books
Beatings with golf clubs
Feigned optimism
Exploitable weaknesses
Things that would have been funny if they
    hadn't happened to you
Being commanded to be charming
Little Big Man (the movie)
Little Big Horn (the battle)
Tourists in Florence
People who confuse beauty with virtue
Affectations
Annual displays of affection for your mother
Poorly paid tomato pickers
Cursing at inanimate objects
Klinefelter's syndrome—a chromosomal
    abnormality that can cause infertility
Men who are not Marlon Brando
Breakups averted by having sex
Breakups caused by having sex
Failure to communicate
Mistaking sour cream for whipped cream at
    dinner
Mistaking sour cream for whipped cream in
    bed
Neighborhoods where sodas are three times
    more expensive than usual
Persuasive nihilists

Wet blankets (metaphorical)

Wet blankets (literal)

Nightmares about exes

People who hog the blankets

Artful dodgers

Shared dental floss

Muddles

The waning of joy

Buses that drive off cliffs

Occupied territories

Wine "critics"

Abused sincerity

Black cats that can't get adopted from shelters
because people think they're demonic

Black cats that really are demonic

Distractingly attractive coworkers

Coupon clipping

The five-second rule

Drinking cheap vodka

Paying for expensive vodka

Brain contusions

Beriberi—a disease caused by vitamin
deficiency

Convulsions

Water torture

The ancient Chinese curse: "May you live in
interesting times"

Tay-Sachs disease

Encopresis—a disorder in which toilet-trained
children pass feces in inappropriate places

Separation anxiety

Brides who ask their bridesmaids to get
cosmetic surgery

Intermittent explosive disorder

Plots that thin rather than thicken

Wishing in vain that a massage would
end in sex

Slobbery kisses

Mustache grooming kits

Expired sunscreen

Eight-year-olds who read sex tip columns in
teen magazines

People who date based on horoscope
compatibility

Glow in the dark deodorant

Speaking French with a Texas accent

Scrawny overworked horses

The smell of cabbage and boiled mutton

Husbands who care less about their wives
than about the TV repairman

People who trust their therapist more than
their spouse

Life-extending foods that you never eat

Helminthic therapy—the increasingly common
practice of treating allergies by introducing
hookworms into the digestive tract

The fact that exercise makes you more
attractive to mosquitoes

Men who love lifting heavy things in front of
women

Friendships based on similar body type
Young Germans who are afraid to ask what their grandparents did
Buyouts
Family-owned stores in rapidly gentrifying areas
Leaving school to marry rich only to be left alone, poor, and ignorant
The fact that only one American president has not presided over combat that engaged troops
The fact that a 300-pound person contains the energy equivalent in fat of 15 gallons of gasoline
Posthole diggers
American-funded insurgents who turn against America
Unsuccessful pranks
Vacuum repairmen
Ideological myopia
Conversion hysteria—the temporary loss of physical functioning due to stress
Journalists who lose their jobs to bloggers
Voters who select a candidate based on likeability
Airlines that charge for soft drinks
Neurosyphilis
The fact that humans don't have ear lids
Exhausted disaster-relief funds
Five hundred year mega-droughts

Scientists paid by tobacco companies to cast
    doubt on evidence that smoking kills
Homes built on geological fault lines
American attempts to exploit ethnic tensions
    in the Middle East
Reviews of porn
Power outages at exotic pet stores
Walk-in closets larger than Manhattan
    apartments
Starvation diets
Being one acquainted with the night
The death of Keats
Baseball fans killed by foul balls
Diapers in the bathtub
Action movies in which the female leads pant
    erotically during combat
Discount divorce lawyers
Doctors who break the Hippocratic oath
Not enjoying food because of nagging
    uncertainty about its nutritional value
Toddlers who try to lift babies and drop them
Trying to politely tell a coworker his feet
    smell
Poems with political agendas
Incomprehensible public transportation
    systems in foreign cities
Ripe apples hanging just out of reach
The awareness that you will never be the best
    at anything you do well
Wet dog smell

Movies on television with commercial breaks
    every five minutes

Nerve damage

Splinters in your eyes

Splinters in your genitals

Cell phone contracts

Sweating profusely in work clothes at 9 A.M.

Discovering your cat's corpse under an
    exterminator's tent

Cleaning up vomit

Pages that fall out of books

Grapes with seeds

Sexual harassment accusations

Walking head-first into a pole

Children who are more adorable than yours

Poop in your briefcase

Modern classical music

Loud, recurring sounds

Finding out you had a chance and lost it

People who bleed on you

Working on holidays

Dropping food in the sand

Overly vigorous anal hygiene

Insufficiently vigorous anal hygiene

Cutting off your nose to spite your face

Your boss greeting you with a command

Being told you should be more like your wife's
    friend's husband

Having money but no time

Having time but no money

Having neither time nor money

Canned cheeseburgers

Insufficiently crisp pickles

Partisan politics

Making the same mistake over and over

Trucks that beep when they back up

The depressive stage of drunkenness

Out-of-tune French horn players

Wobbly tables

Applause while the orchestra is still playing

Fat people with chicken legs

The people who booed Jackie Robinson

Having a little salad with your dressing

Shell companies, whose sole purpose is to acquire other companies

Apartments that are larger than yours but cost less

Fake antiques

Mr. Rogers

Finding out your friend's number has been disconnected because they're dead

Heart palpitations

Empty cartons in the refrigerator

The taste of battery acid

Heinrich Schenker

Injured rats tracking blood all over your apartment

Cork residue in the wine

Tab cola

Lacking moxie

Spending in a month what you make in a year

Children's soccer coaches who weep after losses

The State Secrets Privilege, which allows the government to stop litigation by invoking national security

Racist children's books from the 1950s

Karl Marx action figures

Novels written by computers

Beliefs that change for the right price

Developing countries forced to accept massive loans at terrible rates

Ugly people in lingerie

Micromanagement

Learning your child is developmentally disabled

The yelp of a kicked dog

Cops who don't take bribes

Cops who do take bribes

Diabetics overdosing on insulin

Sudden bouts of hysteria

Michael Bay

Lost manuscripts

Conductors who think they are God

Busybodies

Wives who prefer their babies to their husbands

Phenylketonuria—a rare genetic disorder necessitating a restricted diet

Pizza parlors named for cruel emperors

Unintentionally adopting someone else's mannerisms

Text messaging in theaters
Showers with uncontrollable temperatures
Affairs that just won't end
Elderly people who have to sit while they
    shower
Deadly explosions in high school chemistry
    classes
Beer that's mostly foam
Gutter balls
Bowling splits
Accidentally shitting yourself
People who think the internet is a physical
    location
Polycystic ovarian syndrome
Homeless shelters that are nicer than
    your building
Neighborhoods with nowhere for children
    to play
Fifty-five-year-old great-grandmothers
Clear-cutting
Churches that get burned down
Kids who ask for food for Christmas
Music majors who hate music
English majors who never read
Coming home to find a smoking pile of rubble
    where your house was
Self-inflicted tattoos
Having sex with someone who just peed
Being selected for additional random security
    screening

Acting helpless for attention
Rooster sex
White people with dreadlocks
Waxy fruit
Fire ants
Nothingness
Chronic flesh-eating diseases
Reruns
Moldy strawberries at the bottom of the carton
Breast-fed four-year-olds
Homes built on Indian burial grounds
Four dollar wine that tastes like gasoline
People who drink milk from the bottle
Children with filthy minds
Cats sleeping on the stove
Dead flies in beer
Velveeta
Bacon bits
Crunchy Jell-O
The death of Bozo the Clown
People who don't know they have HIV
Public flossing
People who pick their noses in their cars
Popsicle stick sculptures
Chintzy folk art
Bad covers of good songs
Grass stains
Eating the stickers on fruit
High socks with tennis shoes
Crab lice

Thumb burns from lighters

Rectal bleeding

Coughs that last for months

Lanyards hawked by Girl Scouts

Airplane toilets during turbulence

Parents who use their teenage children for
style inspiration

Little brothers

Big brothers

Choosing your friends based on their video
games

Death by potato gun

Spam filters that filter out real e-mails

Blood blisters

Eating most of your meals in a car

People who bite when they kiss

Loud country music at 4 A.M.

Forgetting the attachment on an e-mail

Being unable to open the attachment on
an e-mail

Opening the attachment on an e-mail and then
discovering that it's a virus that sends copies
of itself to everyone on your contact list

Having to e-mail everyone on your contact
list to apologize for infecting them with
said virus

Hush money

Aum Shinrikyo, the Japanese cult that carried
out the Tokyo subway attacks

Ripping off a Band-Aid slowly

"Life is good" T-shirts

Being fired with the phrase: "It's time to help you succeed elsewhere"

Granite countertops, which can emit high levels of radiation

Goosebumps

Life in the fast lane

Amber alerts

Overextending yourself

Water cooler conversations

Having to go to the bathroom in the middle of a really good movie

Brainstorming sessions

Job recruiters finding drunken photos of you on social networking sites

Job recruiters finding drunken photos of someone else with your name on social networking sites

Airport workers' strikes

Predictions that airfares will only keep going up

Canceling a planned vacation due to gas prices

Not knowing how much salt to put in recipes that call for "a pinch"

Airlines that charge to redeem frequent flier miles

Hotel prices in major cities

False positives

False negatives

The 400,000 people on the government's terror watch list

Bandwagons
Watching your home equity melt away
Acts of God
The fate of Timothy Treadwell
Gloomy economic forecasts
The mansions of drug lords
Archetypes in teen movies
Prurience
Studies showing that many normal-weight
    teenagers consider themselves fat
Being paid a pittance
Black market iPhones
Overzealous anesthesiologists
Insufficiently zealous anesthesiologists
Pretentious names for paint colors
Getting DVDs from Netflix that are broken in
    half
Doctors who rape their patients
Vagina dentata
Eyebrow mites
Female condoms
The failure of the future to live up to *The Jetsons*
Room temperature tater tots
The flaccid penis
Being sent to bed without dessert
Porridge
Slowly losing your mind
Quickly losing your mind
The royal "we"
Fact-checkers

Sarin gas
L. Ron Hubbard
Roofies
The nickname "ginger" for redheads
Poured concrete
People who use books purely as decoration
The Rapture
Emigration
Postmodernists
Fads
Civil War reenactments
Renaissance fairs
Hummel figurines
Commemorative plates
Decoupage
White people co-opting black culture
Crop circles
OPEC
Florid psychosis
Anachronistic acronyms
Widgets
Saboteurs
Mistaking hallucinogenic mushrooms for
    regular mushrooms
Mistaking regular mushrooms for
    hallucinogenic mushrooms
Rasputin
Xerxes—an ancient Persian king who was
    stabbed to death
Excuses not to shower

Helvetica font
Player haters
Basic cable
German air strikes against all the British
  cities featured in *Baedeker's Guides* during
  World War II
Roughing it
Derivative plots
Unnecessary kitchen gadgets
Fund-raising telethons
Condom vending machines
Exploding carbonated beverages
Video games that inspire movies
Jerry Bruckheimer
Jazz squares
Jazz hands
Bad caviar
Unread obituaries
Anal sex in trailers
Street fiddlers
False truisms
Maundering
Pandering
The fact that one in five U.S. bridges is over
  fifty years old, the maximum age for which
  they were designed to be safe
Commuting in Tokyo
Callow youth
Ichthyosaur fan clubs
Discreet murmurs of disapproval

Racist grandmothers

Lack of consent of the governed
Descartes' evil deceiver
Enormous belt buckles
Being drawn and quartered
Believing yourself to be charming
The limits of kindness
False summits
Sentimental moments in action movies
Opening fire on civilians
Towns with populations of forty-seven
Surreys with the fringe on top
Girls who can't say no
Recidivism
One-sided documentaries
Last rites
Loveless marriages
Dipsomaniacs
Dying in a motel room
The ends of honeymoons
Strategic crying
Being mistaken for your mother
Sullen porters in French hotels
Homes swallowed by the sea
Grinning and bearing it
Living with people whose death you long for
Uncreative serial killers
Creative serial killers
Parents who define "orgasm" to their four-
    year-olds
Unmemorable last words

Caviar sculptures

Failing to surpass the achievements of your parents

Being crushed in a hydraulic press

Rancid meat at cheap buffets

The frailty of the flesh

Academic quibbling

Failing to flirt your way out of a ticket

Stubbornness

Inexorable declines

Alcoholics' hidden liquor stashes

The hollow men

Being told what to think

Not liking your cellmate

Unappeasable anger

A gray succession of empty days

Daydreaming pilots

Cairns

Dying curses

Dreading the question: "What do you do for a living?"

Children who are never invited to birthday parties

Being unable to recall entire years

Being afraid to take the last chip

Children who learn that daddy has two wives

The blood lust of boxing fans

Claims that universal qualities are national traits

Being over-ready to admit your own faults

Joyless laughter

The shadows of distant rain clouds
Love thwarted by religious differences
Fifth wives
Milk with chunks in it
Profaned temples
Children playing on lawns covered with
pesticides
The despair of the dissolute
The false camaraderie of crowds
www.findachinesebride.com
The invention of the rifle
Vanquished Native American tribes
Shoddy internet research
Being unable to remember the names of all
the people you've slept with
Being unable to remember the names of any
of the people you've slept with
People who giggle at the sight of lesbians
The bloody muzzles of gorging hyenas
Perpetually disappointing your parents
Children who vanish in the night
Falling off ladders
Walking under ladders
Collisions between pedestrians
Fraudulent billing practices
Fainting during yoga
Screaming fights at 3 A.M.
Sharing a table with strangers
Sharing condoms with strangers
Literary jealousy

Dying before your parents do
Using cultural differences to justify infidelity
Deathbeds
The ruined choirs where late the sweet birds
    sang
Long car trips with twelve-year-olds
Swallowing bees while biking
Living beyond your means
Accidentally dropping an air conditioner out
    the window
Children playing with matches
Children running with knives
People who spend more on one meal than
    what other people spend in a week
Romantic overtures misinterpreted as
    friendliness
Friendliness misinterpreted as romantic
    overtures
Children drawing pictures of Nazis
Stingrays
Getting sunburned where the sun don't shine
Cartoon renditions of *Hamlet*
People who think the dawn of civilization
    dates to the dawn of YouTube
Stomping on a kitten
Learning that odors are actually ingested
    matter
People who consider ambivalence weakness
Accidentally pushing your finger through the
    soft spot on a baby's skull

Five-year-olds in SAT prep classes

Having to pee in your McDonald's cup during a traffic jam

The health department closing your favorite Chinese restaurant for serving cat in the stir-fry

Being ordered to leave the museum for touching a fourth century amphora

Losing your husband's grandmother's engagement ring

Losing your husband's grandmother

Parents who tell children their dead relatives are watching them

Little girls making their Barbie dolls have sex

Mothers who encourage their daughters to stuff their bras

Children who know the plot of *All My Children*

When the CEO of your company gets paid 4,200 times more than you

Discussing politics with someone who reads only the comics

Realizing you don't care about endangered birds

Children who are too ugly to put up their pictures

Kids who scribble on your leather furniture

Tickle Me Elmo dolls

Extra chromosomes

Parents whose tempers are worse than their children's

Affected poets who pronounce poem "po-aim"

Parents who accompany their children on
their honeymoon

Feather quills in your chicken

Somalia's GDP per capita, which is the lowest
in the world

Waiting on snobby rich people

Misspelling "happy birthday" on a birthday
cake

Doggy dentists

Rug burns

When your mother remarries an abusive
psychopath

Losing your virginity to a horse

Six-year-olds fascinated by the crucifixion

Hot air from the car's air conditioner

Poodles dyed pink

Last call

Pretentious food critics

The fact that rats can chew through steel

Pinching your eyeball while removing your
contacts

Hamsters in Halloween costumes

Getting shot in the eye with firecrackers

Cell phones breaking

Awkward silences in big groups

Awkward silences on the phone with your
crush

Forgetting your driver's license the day you
get a ticket

Hitting all the red lights on your way to work

Having your name mispronounced at
    graduation
Your parents suing each other
Daughters who baby their mothers
Strangers who stare at you
Young girls who actually think their celebrity
    crush is going to marry them
Distant relatives with crushes on you
Having to choose between your parents
Anorexic men
People who complain about the upkeep of
    their beach houses
Finishing books that suck just to finish them
Loud bongo drums that give you a headache
Having no relief
Having no release
Neighborhood crazies who bring their dogs to
    the post office
Cute kids who know how much they can get
    away with
Ugly kids who know they can't get away with
    much
Blind birds
Young children who tell you that their dad is
    in the closet
Fitness centers with no ventilation
Weeks clogged with doctors appointments
People whose simple pleasures include private
    jets and home theaters
Yoga studios near highways

People with no rhythm who take dance classes
Getting someone else's order
Receiving obviously cheap gifts
Eating and running
The urge to pee during sex
Nickelodeon
Teenage girls who call their mom lame
People who resemble their pets
Having the runs at a family party
Skinny pigs
Old men who don't trim their ear hair
Liver spots
Five-year-olds who dominate dinner
    conversations
People who teach foreigners highly offensive
    phrases
Grim librarians
People stressed out about planning their
    vacations
Bloody and swollen piercings
People who don't know what sex is until they
    have it
Larynx cancer
Explaining sex positions to middle-aged people
People who laugh at everything
People who laugh at nothing
Incorporating food into your daily
    masturbation routine
Soda addiction
Being the drunkest person in the room

Tripping as you walk down the aisle
Advertisements that stick in your head
Germ-infested shawls
Holes in the fuselages of jet liners
Acoustic neuroma—a nerve tumor in the head
People who have their whole lives ahead of
    them
Weeping on the grave of your hopes
Fidgeting
Cancer of the parotid
Wandering and suffering on the barren sea
Theodicy
Secretly enjoying funerals
Biking off a mountain and dying
Cruelty caused by the desire to be manly
Contaminated aquifers
Conditional love
Subtle bias in the media
Aegisthus—a Greek hero born of an incestuous
    union between a father and his daughter
Not being able to hold a yoga pose for more
    than five seconds
Fawns in the lairs of lions
Offending the gods
Bellies cramped with hunger
Rigged horse races
Doctors who answer their cell phones while
    performing surgery
The uneasy dreams of rats
Ancient blood curses

Hearing your coffin being made outside the
    window of the room in which you're dying
Deals tied up in escrow
Anorexics at the gym
Babies fed raw meat
Obituaries that misspell the name of the
    deceased
Penguins waddling to a certain death
People waddling to a certain death
Sniffing lighter fluid
Stopping for a yellow light and then realizing
    you could have made it
Older siblings who tell you you're adopted
    (when it's not true)
Older siblings who tell you you're adopted
    (when it is true)
Bilge
People who get violently competitive when
    playing croquet
People in countries with governments that
    prohibit travel
Lungs full of saltwater
The sighing of the wind
Laws that allow landlords to displace tenants
    in rent-stabilized apartments
Dying atheists whose Christian families insist
    on religious funerals
Dying Christians whose atheist families insist
    on nonreligious funerals
Compulsive reading of obituaries

Eulogies read from flashcards
Pushing wheelchairs uphill
Little people on trampolines
Ping-Pong injuries
Toddlers who insist on playing peek-a-boo
     for hours
Drowned ducklings
Children who hyperventilate while sobbing
Phthalates in children's toys
Jackrabbit sex
Hair styles inspired by the plumage of cockatiels
Economic incentives to break fair labor laws
Accidentally blowing up your commanding
     officer
Intentionally blowing up your commanding
     officer
Worthless warranties
Products that break just after the warranty
     expires
Depending on unreliable people
Friendships ruined by failed business ventures
Hired thugs who gun down union leaders
Thin squirrels that won't survive the winter
The sickly afternoon moon
Spitting into the wind
Peeing into the wind
Big countries that get mad at small countries
     for trying to be like them
People who belch and then tell you it's good
     manners in China

Religious leaders whose jowls swing when
they move their heads
Friends who take you to a karaoke bar
The smell of men's T-shirts in a Greyhound
Bus station
The smell of urine in a nursing home lobby
The word "putrid"
Colliding with automatic doors
People who say "borrow" when they mean
"take"
Your grandmother thinking you're a slut
Bicyclists who fall over while balancing at red
lights
Getting a stepfather when you're fifty
Watching someone else take the last free
sample
Knowing you sound stupid but continuing to
talk anyway
The lips of Medusa
Bribed health inspectors
Visionaries in asylums
When you can no longer afford to be picky
Photographs of bloody soldiers smiling next
to their dead enemy
The universally despised
Food lobbyists who skew the food pyramid
Uninhabited mansions
Contradictory advice from different doctors
When following your intuition leads to a
violent death

The Joker

People who chronically underpay when eating out in groups

Finding the expensive gift you gave someone sitting on a shelf in their garage

Weird bedfellows

Repeat offenders

Second homes

Third homes

Fourth homes

Children who drown in their own swimming pools

Feeling as though you've swallowed a wolverine

Chasing the ice cream truck but not catching it

Knowing how long you have left to live

Open auditions

Poorly marked detour routes

Wedding gowns bought at Wal-Mart

People who repeat other people's jokes

Babysitting demonic infants

Doorbells that play college fight songs

Eerily human automated voices

Formulaic expressions of sympathy

A deepening sense of the inexpressible

Weirdly shaped baby heads

Learning your wife was once known as "the tamer of men"

Downed helicopters

Friendships based on the desire to sound impressive

Apostates condemned to eternal doom
Lost first editions
Joseph
Supreme Court justices who just can't recall
    which one the Second Amendment is
Roasting marshmallows on the edge of an
    active volcano
Movies that use their length to compensate
    for their quality
Dead soldiers left on battlefields
Finding your parents' stash of hallucinogens
Not having enough bullets to kill your enemy
Not having enough bullets to kill yourself
Having your children shoplift for you
People who consider getting high an act of
    political protest
Your girlfriend picking her nose and wiping it
    on you
Crushes on waitresses that you never do
    anything about
Cathedrals with entry fees
Factory dormitories for workers
The dwindling tiger population in India
Clan wars caused by a pig that ruined a garden
Goats' breath
Geniuses who can't dress themselves
Not getting enough protein
People who make fun of foreign names
Parents who think their teenagers are virgins
Perfect recall of debts and grievances

Couples who never fight
Confiding in the enemy
"Summer" as a verb
Lighting candles around a corpse to ward off
    evil spirits and accidentally setting the
    corpse on fire
Religious poems that compare Jesus to a
    warlord who rapes and pillages the village
    of the soul
Lost lunch boxes
Embarrassingly emotional letters from your
    mother
Mistaking flour for heroin
Mistaking heroin for flour
Getting walked in on while you're going to the
    bathroom
Getting walked in on while you're masturbating
    in the bathroom
Poorly marked speed limits
False starts
Dead deer on the side of the road
Your dog getting sprayed by a skunk
Running a yellow light that turns into running
    a red light
Not being able to get no satisfaction
Being addicted to love
Giving love a bad name
Whipping it good
Being welcomed to the jungle
Sending out an SOS to the world

Total eclipses of the heart
Karma chameleons
Newfangled nicknames for genitals
Not knowing that Vaseline erodes the rubber
   in condoms
Disappointing campfire stories
Trying to visualize infinity
Eating candy off the floor of the movie theater
Putting your arm around the wrong person at
   the movie theater
Snot that moves as you breathe
Being stuck in traffic next to your nemesis
Under-employed actors in theme park animal
   costumes
Six-year-olds who call themselves artists
Men who order daiquiris
Oral sex that takes over an hour to finish
Uncircumcised converts to Judaism
When the fire alarm goes off after you've been
   tied to the bed
Acne poorly disguised with makeup
Teenagers forced to sit at the kids' table
Parents who check their children's MySpace
   profiles
Thirteen-year-olds who brag about getting
   high off corn syrup
Being told you look just like someone who's
   hideous
Middle schoolers who claim they're in love
Jane Fonda

Realizing your thirteen-year-old knows more
    about sex than you do
Chinese imperialists
Canasta
People who take their shoes off at the movie
    theater
The reek of eviscerated hogs
The thud of your child's head hitting the floor
Falling off a mechanical bull
Life before Google
The eye gunk of old dogs
Technological dread
Taking your first senior multivitamin
Sex with a time limit
Pastries from McDonald's
Buboes—pustular inflammations symptomatic
    of the bubonic plague
404 errors
Spyware
Gerbils with Facebook profiles
Squalid restrooms at interstate truck stops
Being at the mercy of country doctors
Feigning interest in your child's new
    computer game
Thinking every noise is your cell phone ringing
Video games that teach children to steal
    things and shoot people
The kids using your favorite blanket as a
    snot rag
Seeing your neighbor peeing in his bushes

Toilets that won't flush

Working on deadline during a blackout

Lazy eyes

Your child practicing his new karate moves
on you

Grave rubbings

Passive women with a thing for controlling
men

Living hours away from the nearest hospital

The government telling you what you're
allowed to do with your body

Hot showers after sunburns

Coming home from vacation pregnant with
the child of a man you'll never see again

Mechanical breathing machines

White tape on DVD cases

People who drive with small babies in their laps

The Westminster Kennel Club dog show

Golfers who sink a put and act like they just
scored a touchdown

Uplifting pictures in the terminal patients
wing of the hospital

The carnal desires of the Duchess of York

Idolatry of the Kennedys

Men who compensate for the size of their
penis with the size of their car

Knowing that tomorrow will be just as terrible
as today

Parts of the country that can sustain only one
bookstore for hundreds of miles

Surprise performance evaluations

People who think baseball is a metaphor for life

Manmade bodies of water

When your young child wakes up just as
you're falling asleep

Children of teenage mothers who become
teenage mothers

Botched eye surgery

Comfort that depends on the suffering of
others

Topics of conversation that invariably lead to
screaming fights

Insects that fly up your nose

Trying to drag race an unmarked cop car

People who do a sloppy job committing suicide

Having to pay a toll to get to your own house

Cars with fewer than four wheels

People with multiple homes who cheat on
their taxes

Parents who pick their children's nose

Page after page of "simple" instructions

Young mothers holding a baby in one hand
and a cigarette in the other

Dinky strip mall towns named for European
capitals

Iconic rock 'n' roll stars who are aging just
like everyone else

Cats with no tails

Tube socks

Beginning oboe players

Preachers who will only refer to sex as
  fornication
People who let off steam by hitting animals
Going hunting while drunk
Botflies, which lay their eggs under human flesh
Suing your friends
Canine ear infections
Obese pugs
Wonder Bread
The Florida Tomato Growers Exchange, which
  has blocked a penny-per-pound raise for
  migrant workers
YouTube videos of people playing video games
First-degree burns
Second-degree burns
Third-degree burns
Being so thirsty that you drink your own urine
Not realizing an animal is stuffed
Star Wars conventions
Overlooked talents
Angola, which has the highest infant mortality
  rate in the world
Dogs that don't come home
Letting your child play on the stove
Body parts removed with pliers
Fresh juice from concentrate
People who say "fudge" instead of "fuck"
Buddhists on death row
People who fly to other countries to go shopping
Terrible writers who sell millions of books

Broken headphones
Broken homes
Hot coffee on hot days
Hunters who don't eat what they kill
People with SUVs who complain about gas
    prices
Spending more time on airplanes than at home
Women barred from the priesthood
The self-loathing of overweight ballerinas
Having to hear your eight-year-old practice
    the violin
Children who kick sand on people at the beach
Recognizing your ideas in a friend's book and
    not getting credit for them
Being unable to fill the Tom Cruise–shaped
    hole in your heart
People who get paid lavishly for behaving in
    ways that are condemned by their mothers
Poorly funded cancer research labs
Children incapable of deriving enjoyment
    from anything that isn't plugged in
Self-proclaimed sexologists
Lynched babies
People who want grandchildren but not children
People who live unusually long lives full of poor
    health, hard work, and general suffering
Love based on ignorance of your beloved's
    true character
Optimism based on false information
Servants replaced by laptops

Maddeningly smug technocrats

Self-interest

Useless literary types

Prisoners executed just before DNA results
would have exonerated them

Newspapers that summarize astoundingly
complex issues in a sentence

Authors whose greatest ambition is to bore
future generations with their prose

When the media smells blood

Child actors who lack the good sense to stop
acting before puberty

Close-ups of people's feet

People who kiss the way a horse eats

False modesty mistaken for the real thing

Managers who disguise their own weaknesses
and magnify yours

Hating your own flaws in others

Not being invited along on the crime spree

Politicians with short, selective memories

Surgeons with a flair for improvisation

Disliking in fact people whose rights you
support in principle

People who find your suffering sort of
endearing

Prodigious talents in useless areas

Being in love with a member of a different
species

People more concerned with their comfort
than with your survival

Feeling guilt for the crimes of others

Fights over baby names that end marriages

Writers whose talents ebb with age

The overuse of the word "sizzling" in fast food commercials

Men who mention their salary on first dates

Toilets without toilet seats

Learning your husband's real name from someone who isn't your husband

Confusing the words "philanderer" and "philanthropist"

Confusing the words "incest" and "incense"

The word "stool"

Middle-aged fathers with dating profiles on the internet

Countries to which travelers must bring their own food

Grandpas in Speedos

Alcoholics who pose as wine connoisseurs

CEOs nostalgic for feudalism

Bosses who force their workers to run errands during their lunch hour

Employees forced to pay for their own office supplies

Indecisive jurors

People who subscribe to magazines in order to display them on their coffee table

Fruit juice with more sugar than fruit

Bosses who don't realize they are universally despised

Bosses who blame you for failing to meet
unreasonable expectations that were never
made clear

Readers of financial self-help books who go
bankrupt

New computers that don't work

Being unable to get a loan

Old women massaging their feet in public

Kayakers sucked over massive waterfalls

Spoiled brats who are constantly getting
"loans" from their parents

The embarrassing siblings of famous politicians

Herbicide planes that miss their targets and
dump toxic chemicals into neighborhoods

Politicians who surround themselves with
children and minorities whenever possible

The Roman emperor Caligula's horse Incitatus,
which was a member of the Roman senate

Animals with more elaborate funerals than
people

Hearing that your spouse wants a divorce
from their new lover

Myiasis—a maggot infestation of the human
body

Infants dropped down trash chutes

Abel

Going to Burger King on prom night

Being named River

Overgrazing

Mealy peaches

Tithing
Teething
Barbaric yawps
Obligatory patience
Scalped settlers
Battles between people without guns and
    people with guns
People who pronounce "timbre" like timber
Older men prowling bars
"Für Elise"
Not fitting in your childhood bed
Reading about yourself in someone else's diary
Getting an erection during a massage
Wine critics
Nipples visible beneath shirts
Excessive use of French phrases in conversation
Inordinate grief at the death of movie stars
Unemotional mourning
Hysterical mourning
Guessing someone's ethnicity incorrectly
Wild temperature fluctuations
Relatives killed in distant disasters
Children's books about the Holocaust
The use of "Machiavellian" as a synonym
    for evil
Ballerinas who actually look like the ones in
    Degas paintings
Being rejected by a community college
Rooming with a coke addict
Lactic acid

Meeting people who have slept with your
    husband
Needing more than you're needed
Strollers without brakes
Children impaled on scissors
Death by flamethrower
Girls whose legs have a five o'clock shadow
Musical greetings on answering machines
Bat guano
Poultry farms
Genetic predisposition to mental illness
Kids who prefer McDonald's to lovingly
    home-cooked meals
Improv comedy shows that are actually scripted
International corporations with booths at the
    local farmers' market
Using your hand as an umbrella
Stage mothers
Shirts that say "Hottie" in glittery letters
The gloom of toilet stalls
Being the only girl in the family
Digging a hole to shit in
People who exploit the welfare system
The bottom of a parakeet cage
When no one in your family comes to your
    graduation
Power based on notoriety
Diabolic porcupines
Long-range arrows
Garage sales after evictions

Mar-a-Lago

Doritos breath

Fundamentalists embroiled in sex scandals

The phrase "virile member" in romance novels

The "fatal loins" of the Montagues and the
Capulets

Riding lawnmowers

The Love Canal disaster, in which neighborhood
residents were poisoned by toxic waste

Makeup that all wears off by the end of the
work day

Packing tape

Liquor boxes without lids

Morning-after mascara

Highlights that grow out

Loving the smell of napalm in the morning

People who go around saying "I'm ready for
my close-up"

People who do handstands every morning

Cats named Fluffy

People who steal elephant tusks

"My Heart Will Go On" by Celine Dion

Fake gemstone jewelry

Bleach strips for teeth

The steeplechase

The golf channel

People who constantly say "I hear what you're
saying"

Newscasters who smile at the beginning of
each new story

Full-body casts
Artificial faces
Cyclops
Cleaners that rip the buttons off dress shirts
Calculators that are too complicated to
    actually add and subtract
Artificially distressed wood
People who think they can't live without
    bamboo flooring
Male gym teachers who go by the name "coach"
Bald men who sport heavy beards to make up
    for it
Feng shui
Forty-five-year-old Italian men who still live
    with their mothers
Fox hunting
Small children who pull the legs off frogs
Trompe l'oeil
Trying to pronounce "trompe l'oeil"
Peeling wallpaper
Very old liberals
Chipped Christmas balls
Roger Moore as James Bond
Huge white plastic jewelry
Drought in the west
Cheetos
Mine tailings
Coagulated curds
Pine beetles
Pilgrimages undertaken on your knees

Rural dentistry
Baseball games canceled due to rain
High wind warnings
Missile silos
Defunct power plants
Familial hypercholesterolemia
Pauper's graves
Cow patties
The death of Mercutio
Huts that are lit on fire so that the inhabitants
    can be speared as the smoke forces them
    outside
Gristle

Soap scum

Capsized canoes
Hairballs
A cow's cud
Nuns with record deals
Fluorescent hunting vests
Swimming with snapping turtles
Reading your doom in a goat's entrails
Children's songs played on repeat during long
    car trips
Products with "some assembly required"
Scrub brushes
Substituting travel videos for travel
Spirochetes—the bacteria which cause
    syphilis and Lyme disease
Horses dying of colic
Antique pistols that you didn't think would
    actually fire

Being judged by your choice of font
People with easy lives who hire personal
    assistants
Old women in short skirts
Little girls in short skirts
Sniffing glue
Walking in on your secretary shooting up in
    the bathroom
Losing your boss' personal files
Loud, overly air-conditioned coffee shops
People who use plastic bags instead of condoms
Birth control pills that kill your sex drive
Homophobes in urban areas
Homophobes in rural areas
Feeling misrepresented by the person who
    knows you best
Psychotic spouses
Plastic bags that replace broken car windows
Young children who know more than you
Kids who are more interesting than their
    parents
Coworkers who went to more prestigious
    colleges than you
Realizing you don't like any of your friends
Being asked personal questions at interviews
People who look at you and your parents and
    ask if you are adopted
Offices without windows
Offices without walls
People who find *Sex and the City* profound

Weird marks on your face that won't go
away and force you to make dermatology
appointments

Your mom's weekly e-mails letting you know
who died

Starbucks employees who can't afford to get
coffee at Starbucks

Neighborhoods with no soul

Fighting with your boyfriend while
surrounded by happy couples

Wanting to live somewhere that your spouse
hates

Boyfriends who refuse to wash their faces and
cut their hair

Having buyer's remorse after your adopted
child arrives

When your boyfriend describes how great his
life used to be before you were in it

When you think soreness is temporary
but it isn't

Baristas who sing out coffee orders

When your father-in-law has a crush on you

Getting all your ideas about gay people from
Will & Grace

Shrinks who doodle instead of taking notes
during therapy sessions

People who think they're more famous than
they actually are

The weekly trip to your husband's grave

Confusing "to" and "too"

Confusing "there," "their," and "they're"

Confusing "then" and "than"

Confusing "further" and "farther"

The day your boss comes back from vacation

Stepmothers jealous of their stepdaughters

Coffee shops with abstract paintings of coffee mugs

When your overweight friends ask you if they're too fat

Opera singers who crack on their high notes

Realizing that you said too much about something that isn't even your business

People who refuse to work with people of different races or genders

When stretching really hurts

People who talk about their BlackBerrys all the time

Grease 2

Kids singing explicit songs without knowing what the words mean

When someone tries to flirt with you while you're trying to work out

Pressing CUT instead of COPY and losing your work

World music playing at Starbucks

Having nobody to watch your stuff so you can go to the bathroom at the coffee shop

The urge to shit after drinking coffee

People who are proud of never leaving their neighborhoods

Businessmen in really tight suits

Being the oldest kid at summer camp

Being the only boy in the school play

People who are proud of being bitter

Women who gleefully warn you how bitchy
they are

Twelve-year-olds who think they aren't virgins
because they have cybersex

Getting terrible birthday gifts from your
husband every year

When everyone in your office is thin and
attractive

People who ask you what's wrong with
your face

Alcibiades, who led the Spartans in battle
against his former Athenian countrymen

Alfonso IX, King of Léon, nicknamed "the
Slobberer"

Nigerian e-mail scams

The Pentagon's attempts to develop a gay
bomb, which would promote homosexual
behavior among enemy troops

Imelda Marcos, former first lady of the
Philippines, owner of 3,400 pairs of shoes

The 230 foot rise in global sea levels that
would result from the melting of all the ice
in Antarctica

Smells that travel through thick walls

People who consider football a form of
spirituality

Getting stupider over time
Seduced and abandoned chambermaids
Bribes disguised as gifts
Vietnam Village—a 1976 Florida theme park
    that recreated a ravaged village during
    the war
Feminist critics who describe Emily
    Dickinson's style as "clitoral"
Failed attempts to flatter your professor
Failed attempts to fellate your professor
Paper airplane crashes
Teachers who refuse to hold class outside
People who rely on machines for happiness
Getting caught by a janitor while hooking up
    in the college library
Being honest about your mistakes and getting
    punished for them anyway
When the prison rejects your request for a
    single cell
Drinking from a broken glass
Failed attempts to open beer bottles in
    dramatic ways
Mascots attacked by rabid fans
Corpses with eyelids frozen shut
Teachers who divide students into the "the
    bad" and "the worse"
Your boyfriend requesting that you shave your
    pubic hair
European soccer riots in which a fairly shocking
    number of people die or are trampled

Hockey fans hit in the head with the puck
People who send thank-you notes after hookups
Trying to eat dinner for under a dollar
People who say "I hate to do this" but then do it anyway
Foods that come in crinkly bags
Bathing at the car wash
People who do laundry annually
When your roommate is having more sex than you
Airplane pilots with drinking problems
Curtains made from newspapers
Students who pick colleges based on nearby bars and clubs
Pigeons killed with brooms
Losing your wedding ring down the disposal
Dumbbells dropped on toes
Escaped lobsters
Meals made up of condiments
People who constantly buy new cell phones
Parents who don't seem to realize their baby's diaper needs changing
Being dumped because your lover hates your parents
Attempts to bond with random housemates who already have enough friends
Trying to distinguish Monet from Manet
Overpaid tutors who don't make your children any smarter
Rapists who don't really see what the big deal is

Medical students allowed to practice on the
    uninsured
Winning because you cheated
Claiming your grandma died to get out of
    an exam, then having her actually die a
    week later
Being served by the waitress you forgot to tip
    last time
Self-styled playas who are actually in
    monogamous relationships
Heirs to great wealth who claim to have made
    their own fortunes
Jurists killed by the accused's hitman
The beaten path
Taking the road not taken and getting eaten
    by a grizzly
Shaved heads that look like bullets
Running out of money in a country where you
    don't speak the language
Being gored by an elephant tusk
Being ready for Friday by Tuesday
Graffiti artists with poor penmanship
Finding out the town where you were born is
    now a superhighway
Garbage men described as "waste disposal
    specialists"
Feeling responsible for someone's suicide
Revealing someone's major health problems
    to a mutual friend
Tranquilizing your dog after driving it crazy

Aggressive shoe shiners

Reminding people that they owe you money

People who keep porn in the bathroom

People who claim to have read *Finnegan's Wake*

Corpse-sniffing dogs

Only children whose request for a sibling is never granted

Men's bathrooms with no partitions between the urinals

Children who suddenly develop speech impediments

Insincere apologies

Doctors who exchange pleasantries with you before they tell you that you have terminal cancer

Colon cleanses

Fingers broken during dodge ball

Adults who play competitive tag

People who treat their personal assistants like shit

Getting stuck in the car wash

Taking a convertible through the car wash

Trying to cook for a chef

Tourette's syndrome

Moments of repose ruined by screaming children

Waking to the sound of jackhammers

Dogsled teams that crash through thin ice and die

Racehorses killed by the Mafia

People who stop learning once they finish school

Having to accept cuddling instead of sex

People who insist on wearing two condoms

Men who think hugging another man is proof of homosexuality

People who call out their own name during sex

Your boyfriend asking to borrow your lipstick

Human heads stored in the freezer

Flunking your court-ordered anger management classes

Trading pot for sex

Trading sex for pot

Men with the word "Mom" tattooed on their ass

Urinating forty times a day

Monogrammed bathrobes

The Sundarbans mangrove forest in Bangladesh, where Bengal tigers kill as many as eighty people a year

Children who play "the choking game"

People who clean their guns near your head

Constantly suspecting that you have an STD

Car windows getting smashed in the winter

Being told your girlfriend is pregnant

Pants worn just below the ribcage

People who finish your sentences for you

Noisy finger-licking during a meal

Being whacked in the head with a rolled-up newspaper

Chefs with violent coughs
People who crash into your parked car and
  leave an illegible note
Dates who want to show you their machete
  collections
Lumberjacks crushed by falling trees
Coworkers who betray you
Receiving mouthwash as a gift
Acquaintances who ask to crash at your place
  for a few weeks
Dogs bathed in the kitchen sink
Cigarette ashes dropped on furniture
Parents who disown their children
Children who disown their parents
Biting your nails
Getting arrested while skinny-dipping
Crashing a borrowed car
Strobe lights in private homes
Sudden weight gain after marriage
Worms crawling from eye sockets
Halloween costumes made of garbage bags
People who are famous because they're
  related to famous people
Being introduced to your son
Always ordering more than you can eat
Thinking *Hedda Gabler* is a rare species of
  turkey
Crampon wounds
Young actors influenced by Sylvester Stallone
Inbred tigers with learning disabilities

Motorized walking sticks
Delayed breast development
Dunderheads
Gastric disturbances
Weddings with corporate sponsors
Stained wedding dresses
Escaped hamsters
People who want to see letters of
    recommendation before they'll date you
Lords who flick cigar ash onto smiling servants
Broken strands of pearls
Hairstyles that take hours
Having so much to confess that the priest asks
    to finish the session tomorrow
People who are allergic to flowers
Dropped birthday cakes
Grooms too drunk to consummate the
    marriage
Monsoons during the honeymoon
Mothers given an ironing board for Mother's
    Day
Waist-deep snow
"Fixer uppers"
Atrophic vaginitis—a painful condition that
    causes burning and itching in the vagina
The Death Zone—the area above 26,000 feet
    on Mount Everest
Aron Ralston, who amputated his own arm to
    escape from beneath a huge boulder
The annual deforestation rate in Brazil

The death stalker scorpion, the most venomous scorpion in the world

Passing boats that don't see the desperate arm-waving of shipwreck victims

The annual deforestation rate in Brazil

Dengue fever

Rafflesia, a flower with the scent of a rotting carcass

The giant black tiger snake

Mary Ward, the first ever motor vehicle accident victim in 1869

Eating to fill the void within

Not having exact change

Losing a snowball fight

Amateur attempts at gutting a hog

Not missing your children at all when they grow up and move away

People who watch other people get mugged and don't do anything

Getting over a long and serious relationship in a disturbingly short time

Dating an amateur artist who is always asking you to pose nude and then sketching unflattering drawings

Knowing that praise and compliments aren't true

People who brag about their sports exploits from previous decades

Parents who are sort of relieved when the kids are taken by Social Services

People who ask God for an iPod

Attempted suicide used as a conversation starter

Knowing that things wouldn't be that different
if you'd never been born

Biographies of vapid celebrities

Stealing flowers from a graveyard and giving
them to your mother

Not losing the weight you gained during
pregnancy

Ulcerative colitis—a condition that causes
rectal bleeding and the sudden need to use
the bathroom

Bosses who are nasty in e-mails but pleasant
in person

Failing kindergarten

Grins of suppressed bitterness

Politicians who declare shopping a patriotic duty

Collection agencies that try to collect debts
from the deceased

Cyberbegging

Skid marks on roads

Skid marks in underwear

Children who put superglue on toilet seats as
a prank

Hugging your grandmother too tightly and
breaking her ribs

Ball hogs

Getting caught staring at a stranger's genitals

Art teachers who encourage their untalented
students

The desire to inflict your creativity on the world

Persistent attempts to steer the conversation back to yourself

Babies at fine arts museums

Chastity belts

Dying while composing your last great symphony

Infinitely delayed gratification

People who posses all of your strengths and none of your flaws

Surrendering

Refusing to surrender

Soldiers who miss their mothers

Eternal construction projects

Burning cow dung for energy

Realizing that your hard-earned tuition money is allowing your daughter to drink beer, have sex, and skip class

Carrying water in a sieve

The roaming ghosts of the unburied dead

Accidents with meat cleavers

Priests who doze off while listening to confessions

Friendships ruined by living together

Murder in the town square

Con artists who cheat the elderly out of their life savings

Minority writers who are assumed to speak for their entire race

Bad moods that last for years

Being deemed unnecessary

Homes with movie theaters

Seizure-inducing music

Needing a permit to have a dog

Recycled Christmas gifts

Journalists with delusions of political influence

Philanthropists who live in mansions

Ecstatic self-wounding in pre-Christian
religious rituals

Dirigibles

Being charged for an international call that
was a wrong number

Thirteen-year-olds getting nose jobs

Choking on vitamin pills

People who are willing to pay you for a urine
sample

Feeling compelled to tell someone they did a
good job

Romanticizing urban life

Romanticizing rural life

The forthcoming opera version of Al Gore's
An Inconvenient Truth

Using the word "ridiculously" to modify
complimentary adjectives

Meeting your new boyfriend at your
husband's funeral

People who leave meaningful jobs to get MBAs

Little girls who dream of being flight attendants

Having a passion for office supplies

Inheriting a failing family business

Impasses
Realizing your greatest epiphanies were just
      random connections between cortical
      circuits
Smushed sandwiches

Funeral urns

Hard day's nights
Day trippers
Tickets to ride
Nowhere men
Long and winding roads
Trying to outrun a forest fire
The success rate of relationships from
      The Bachelor
People who call parties "soirees"
Morning breath
Couples who finish each other's sentences
Roscoe the miniature donkey
General Hospital
Hearing about how well your ex is doing
Noticing your lover yawning during sex
When you can tell by the sound of someone's
      voice that they have awful news
The fact that Florida has twice as many
      lightning casualties as any other state
Electroencephalographic abnormalities
Pulmonary edema—fluid accumulation in the
      lungs
Tinnitus—a constant ringing in the ears
Hair braided too tight
Dogs killed by alligators

In vitro fertilization

Beating your own drum

Children who are terrified on Halloween

Wealthy people with multiple nannies

Changelings

Getting drunk off Listerine

Celebrities who found charities as PR stunts

Kevin Federline

The abduction of Jean Paul Getty by kidnappers who subsequently cut off his ear

Adult swim

Going hog wild

Kissing and telling

Making your grandmother cry

Unhappy campers

Forgetting to pack your child's Ritalin on vacation

Opening acts

Your teenager racking up an immense phone bill

The pretense of certainty

Defection

Teachers who are afraid to touch their students for fear of sexual harassment charges

People who see you with your boyfriend and say incredulously: "Wow, you two are still together?"

Twelve-year-olds with iPhones

Rich people who shop at the Salvation Army

Feeling self-conscious about the size of your car

Being put out to pasture

Amateur tattoo artists

Chopping off all your hair after a breakup

Hobbled donkeys

Photos of people singing with their mouths wide open

Treacle

Political speeches about people uniting and walls coming down

Staticky hair

Feature-length infomercials

Campers singing "Kumbaya"

Trying to read Schopenhauer on the toilet

Failed attempts to get fired

People who hover without participating in conversations

Sanitized media portrayals of war

People who really should be wearing clothes

Dress shoes with shorts

Fighting in Sadr City

Flunking a wine tasting course

Organic deodorants that don't work

Hostage negotiations

Tariffs

Keraunopathy—pathology caused by being struck by lightning

Companies with terrible customer service that monitor your calls for quality assurance

People who see dosage warnings as a challenge

Blowing your diet on the weekends

Young children taking cholesterol-lowering
   drugs
High blood-sugar levels
Low blood-sugar levels
Trying too hard to be fabulous
The 35 million trees killed each year to
   produce American magazines
Shiite refugees in Pakistan
Mortar fire
Vivisection
The average salary of $5.2 million for NBA
   athletes
Ambulances stuck in traffic
Little League players whose parents lie and
   say they're still young enough for the
   sport
Offers for help that are made while drunk and
   rescinded once sober
Starfucking
Sectarian violence
Wishing you had someone else's parents
Low-density lipoproteins
Life after thirty
Taliban training camps
Junk food in school meals
The reek of piss and sweat
Charmed lives
Vulvodynia—vaginal pain so severe you can't
   sit comfortably
Printed retractions

Low self-esteem
High self-esteem
Smarminess
Seeing a relative on *Jerry Springer*
Nonworking fireplaces
The relationship between Harlem residents
    and the NYPD
Pandora's box
Night riders
Knight Rider
Embassy bombings
Guilt by association
Sleep deprivation
Little orphan Annie
Apartments that need multiple locks
Children who rip open gifts without reading
    the cards
Breaking up in a foreign country
Backlash
Being bushwhacked
Milquetoasts
Little boys trying to pee at men's urinals
Not knowing whether Philadelphia is a city or
    a state
Accidentally handing the teller your grocery
    list while trying to rob a bank
Losing a game of tug-of-war
Designing your own tombstone
Unsuccessful snake charmers
Forgetting to pull the rip cord

The sport of dwarf-throwing

Aeschylus, who was killed when an eagle
mistook his bald head for a rock and dropped
a tortoise on it to crack its shell open

Confusing the gas with the brakes

Prisoners executed by being boiled alive

The Keeper of the Heads, who was
responsible for removing the rotting heads
of traitors from London Bridge to make
room for new ones

Divorces caused by bad cooking

Skydivers that land on people

Roller coasters that get stuck while everyone's
upside down

Controlled forest fires that get out of control

Laszlo Toth, who attacked Michelangelo's
Pietà with a sledgehammer

Wanting to buy all the puppies at the pet store

Jean-Michel Basquiat's death which was
caused by choking on his own vomit

Precious childhood mementos sold at garage
sales

Cancellation fees

Relieving yourself on an electrical pole

Spear carriers

Congressmen who fall asleep during House
debates

Smoking guns

Nephritis

Low sodium diets

ApoE4, a protein that predisposes people to
    Alzheimer's disease
Mink turned into fur coats
Spitting competitions
Scleroderma—a chronic, discoloring skin
    disease
Thumbscrews
Boom boxes at the beach
The hamster dance
Children forced to take music lessons
Involuntary cohabitation
Putting a purse on the floor, which means bad
    luck
The low accuracy of lineups for identifying
    criminals
Whoopee cushions
Toxic bachelors
Hamburgers made from sacred cows
The kidnapping of the Lindbergh baby
Speed dating
Ideas that seemed good at the time
Pseudoscience
The Shaver Mystery—a theory that inside
    the earth is a race of detrimental robots
    who have been responsible for most of the
    great disasters of history
Finding that the Empire State Building is not
    as impressive as you imagined
Pennies dropped from great heights
Imbroglios

Conundrums

The Premillenarians, who were convinced that the Second Coming was imminent in the 1800s

Small potatoes

Auschwitz

Governments whose policy decisions are shaped by their creditors

Magnetic poetry kits

Bread riots

Being forced to dig your own grave

Frozen vegetables

Salt on wounds

Kaddish—the prayer for the dead

Locally owned supermarkets put out of business by chains

The industrialization of farming

Quarantine

Corporations with an encyclopedic knowledge of your personal shopping habits

Illegal hiring practices

Price gouging

The gallows

Workers encouraged to skip breaks to which they're legally entitled

Out-of-season fruit

The fact that $1 billion worth of U.S. government subsidies has gone to support Wal-Mart

Fleas

Marauders

The fact that there are both more starving people and more overweight people in the world than ever before

Hypermarkets—massive stores that sell everything from batteries to produce

Unnoticed hunger strikes

Spiders' eggs

The dust bowl

Exploitative labor practices

Abandoned gas stations

Staggering through snowdrifts

The onset of night

Slaughterhouse workers who eat on the job

Charred tree trunks

Wishing your heart was made of stone

Aluminum siding

Tubercular cattle

Being docked an hour's pay for being one minute late

Being burned in effigy

Men who refer to women as "fine-looking females"

Police captains who own the brothels they pretend to raid

Fort Sumter, where the Civil War began

Torn biohazard suits

Firecake—a tasteless mixture of flour and water

Soldiers without shoes

Anal itching

Humans branded like cows

Moldy raspberries
Leaky faucets
Cell phone billing plans that round up
Rambling voice mails
Children who hate you for conceiving them
Neophobia
Losing the battle to name your child
Hip-hoperas
What remains of your soul
Contemplative scrotum scratching
Addicts escaped from rehab
Eerily hairless men
Having to start a new career when you're
    seventy
Ignoring the bidding of compassion
Men who stuff the crotches of their suits
Florid translations of Virgil
Waiting rooms with waiting rooms
Valley Forge during the Revolutionary War
The smell of wet rotting wood
Medical residents doing their first heart surgery
Boring books about the history of jurisprudence
Using a hammock as a diaper table
Places with more tourists than locals
Being the eleventh most wanted criminal
Braidable armpit hair
Choking on your own spit and dying
Sunstroke
Long yellow fingernails
Getting a fatal skin cancer on your toe

Women's bathing suits that can't contain their
   bodies
Jake Barnes's impotence
Misleading road signs
Being attracted to your kid's babysitter
Having a child as a reaction to your midlife crisis
The cost of your daughter's prom dress
The cost of your daughter's wedding
Cyborgs
The 56 percent of American voters who think
   the presidential race is a waste of time
Being too poor to buy toothpaste
The possibility that deodorant causes cancer
Hating your son-in-law
Preteens who talk about sex without knowing
   what it is
Forty-five minute waits at greasy diners
Being too old for the kids' menu
Overprotective older brothers
Force-feeding your child
Rechargeable batteries that won't charge
Broken record players
Unwanted lemons in your water
Rainstorms when you have holes in your shoes
Hearing people burp in restaurants
Losing a tooth in the schoolyard
Exploding mustard bottles
Old men with dyed hair
Always being cast as the ugly duckling in the
   school play

People who can't handle a different opinion
Senior citizens working at Wal-Mart
Puking up greasy Chinese food
Unappreciative boyfriends
Telling the same joke to different people
Skateboarders run over by buses
Guilty attractions to second cousins
Inhaling coal ash
Soldiers who answer their cell phones during
    battle
Sofas upholstered with the hides of
    endangered species
Inspirational movies in which men find the
    meaning of life through playing bongos
Companies that give themselves awards for
    outstanding customer service
Losing your soul by sneezing
Post-haircut itching
Girls with sideburns
Misjudging the line between tastefully
    provocative and outrageously slutty clothing
Hunters who fail to kill with the first shot
Waking in a cold sweat
Knowing your employees would kill you if
    they could
Research subjects who don't know they're
    research subjects
Magazines about dentistry
The shrinking buying power of food stamps
Unproductive pow-wows

Torturers turned butchers
Butchers turned torturers
Realizing a remark you made has a wildly
sexual second meaning
Not recognizing your mother's voice on the
phone
Dogs who love racing cars and one day get
too close
People who claim to have a monopoly on the
truth
Books of rules for fiction writers
Pretending to be crippled to get pity
Our incomplete transcendence of our animal
nature
Talking to automated phone systems
Kissing in a parking lot and getting run over
Formulaic movies about the apocalypse
Men with passionate attachments to their
mothers
The movie preview voice
Never being able to retire
Cartoons that cause seizures
Little kids who suck at soccer
Generic greetings on postcards
Having to rescue yourself
Overly elaborate salutations
Being outrun by your six-year-old
Children's hospitals
Dead yellow grass
Preteens with anorexia

Catching the neighbors' dog peeing on your
lawn

Catching the neighbors' children peeing on
your lawn

Smooth jazz

Urban cowboys

High deductibles

Reading in dim light

Personality pieces in local papers

Bar mitzvahs that cost more than your house

Living off canned beans

Depressed comedians

Jolly tragedians

High school sweethearts forgotten the first
week of college

Reading the last page first

Corporate cover-ups

System failures

Your boyfriend coming back from vacation
with a new girlfriend

Sex that gets you promoted

The wages of sin

Russian prisoners with tuberculosis

Vodka at 7 A.M.

Faded lettering on old signs

Screen doors slamming in the wind

Padlocked bedrooms

Missing chromosomes

Breaking a promise to yourself not to
masturbate

Failed cloning experiments
Children who chew on rawhide dog bones
Hasty moral judgments of dead people
Misunderstood monsters
Massive corporations pretending to be small
    family businesses
The third rail
Discovering that the mailman is your father
Murderers who are otherwise very pleasant
People with an inimitable sense of style
Being shot with an elephant gun
Scheduled spontaneity
Senile doctors
Cursing at children
Not recognizing the lipstick on your
    boyfriend's penis
People fighting over the same cab
Irreversibly bad haircuts
Fake grief for dead strangers
Beautiful days spent on underground trains
Being put in time out
Bathing your ailing parents
Exorbitant rent
"Up and coming" neighborhoods
Being picked last for dodgeball
The desperate need to scratch yourself
Nosebleeds on new shirts
Stores that hire only attractive people
Failed experiments with homemade parachutes
Crashing your parents' car through a brick wall

Cosmetic surgery past age seventy
Finals week
Strangers who casually mention that they
    have cancer
Faces that are wider than they are long
Ricky Martin
Getting a haircut and not having anyone notice
Suffering fools gladly
Unsung heroes
Ersatz ruins
Margins of error
Dying lightbulbs
People in MENSA
Pushy salesmen
The left side of a bell curve
Old women who kick dogs
Clogging someone else's toilet
Dimly lit restaurants where you can't read the
    menu
McDonald's in hospitals
Misplacing your wife
Rapidly muttered side effects at the end of
    commercials
Malfunctioning defibrillators
Broken guitar strings
Forgetting about Daylight Savings Time
Business meetings
The Lhotse face of Mount Everest
Being unable to leave a message because the
    voice mailbox is full

Losing a button

The early death of blues singer Robert Johnson
Idealists dismissed as lunatics
Siddhartha by Hermann Hesse
Stage actors' salaries
Losing your house in a game of poker
Losing your wife in a game of poker
Doing your child's science project for them
Virginia Woolf drowning herself
Sickly geniuses with unhealthy attachments to
    their mothers
Loud commercials
Old toilets
Inebriated pseudo-intellectuals
People stealing glances at your PIN number
No-income, no-asset loans
The media's exploitation of grief
False dichotomies
Self-starters
Unintentional plagiarists
Intentional plagiarists
Homeless men eaten by dogs
Deceptively happy family photographs
Cultural allusions you don't understand
Sharing a bed with four people
Difficulty swallowing
Self-proclaimed incarnations of Indian gods
Paper tigers
Inane puns in newspaper headlines
Sneakers without socks
Child felons

Massive bugs in the shower
People who constantly wear Ivy League T-shirts
Long conversations about hairstyles
Sculptures made of human excrement
Planning your life around watching your
    favorite TV shows
Bad exchange rates
Billionaires turned politicians
The demotion of Pluto from planet status
Female bodybuilders
Male bodybuilders
Other people gawking at your lover
Open-toed shoes in the rain
Trepanning—a surgical technique that
    involves drilling holes in the skull
Losing your children in a heavy fog
Suits with sneakers
Your wife belching
Endless rants about relationship problems
Dying from a disease you can't pronounce
Friendships based on mutual pity
People who call only when they need
    something
Girls who see Halloween as an excuse to
    dress like a prostitute
Adult braces
People who kiss like golden retrievers
People who kiss golden retrievers
Tumi knives, which were used in ancient Peru
    for human sacrifice

People who use any flat surface as a mirror
Expensive clothes that look cheap
When Mommy and Daddy want to kill
    each other
People who aren't as funny as they think they are
Massive goiters
Your sister's boyfriend
Your brother's girlfriend
Children who have children
Kindergarten admissions tests
Homes on the slopes of volcanoes
Blow jobs with teeth
Whiny men singing about their emotions
Generalizations about gender differences
Chronic ear infections
Fashions inspired by prison uniforms
Rainy days at the beach
The illusion that experience equals wisdom
Seeing your grandparents drunk
Auguries of doom
Hormone replacement therapy
Being kicked in the head by a horse
People whose greatest ambition is to be on TV
Being woken by construction outside your
    window
Learning your parents' erotic nicknames for
    each other
The cringing of habitually beaten dogs
The incomprehensible allusions in T. S. Eliot's
    The Waste Land

People whose first names sound like last names
Health food containers that cause cancer
Permanent stains
Ambulance chasers
Getting gas with the car running
Impoverished workers sending money to
    distant countries
Forty-foot pictures of cheeseburgers on
    billboards
Public masturbation
People who just want to die
Getting your head shaved in preparation for
    brain surgery
Living on a noisy block
Friendly hitting
Unfriendly hitting
Pit vipers
Group projects in which you end up doing all
    the work
Old airplanes
Failing every class except gym
Advertisements above urinals
Decades of accumulated earwax
Illegible handwriting
Overcrowded nature preserves
Strange things growing in the kitchen sink
All of your friends and family members who
    will be dead in fifty years
Delayed train service caused by suicides on
    the tracks

Unusually good behavior after fights
Your daughter's first period
Hot air balloon accidents
Parents who give their kids money for getting
    good grades
Muttering rapidly while pacing in circles
Profusely sweating lawyers with bulging eyes
Stolen wheelchairs
Manicured lawns
Dogs with dementia
Last-minute packing
Nonalcoholic beer
Swing voters who determine elections
Purple dog booties
Radium watch dial painters who died of
    radiation poisoning
Stolen pens
Knowing a lot about a little
Knowing a little about a lot
Rarely inspected elevators
The effect of spell check on spelling ability
Husbands with an aversion to yard work
Everything you could accomplish if you
    slept less
Middle-aged people using obsolete slang
Undiscriminating palettes
Discriminating palettes
Falling barometer needles
Being abandoned by the muse
People who call food "cuisine"

Different versions of events

Shattered moments of repose

Streetwalkers

Learning as competition

People from your past who somehow became
  successful

Losing touch with old friends

Palliative care

Dying before having children

Dying after having children

Latent possibilities

Broccoli-flavored chocolate (this actually exists)

Marrying the wrong person

Being too tired for sex

The solitude of an alpine winter

Murals about peace in violent neighborhoods

Doomed transatlantic voyages

Forgetting brilliant ideas

Inarticulate longings

Realizing your enemies have redeeming
  qualities

Messages in bottles that never wash up on
  shore

Wood-chopping accidents

Poor people who spend like rich people

Rich people who spend like poor people

Kids who find the gun closet

Mysterious gurgling in the water pipes

Murphy's Law

People who refuse to validate your feelings

Watching unattractive neighbors undress

Dropping trash into the trashcan without
putting in a garbage bag first

The number of cows killed to make a leather
sofa

Creaky old furniture

Poets turned anarchists

Fitful dreams

Ezra Pound's *The Cantos*

Musty rooms in old basements

The fact that evil people don't have horns

Having no one to share your joy with

Knowing you're not alone in a dark room

Flotsam

Jetsam

Vilifying your victims

Abraham

Isaac

People who frown while thinking

Slag heaps

The scraping of metal on metal

Leaving for work before the sun has risen

Returning from work after the sun has set

Sickly pallor

Surfers who actually use the word "radical" as
a term of praise

Gory chronicles of ancient wars

Knowing more than your doctor

Public spanking

Indiscreet underwear adjustments

Attempts to reverse aging
Living by the sword
Dying by the sword
Yet another day of work
Ordure
Aggressive squirrels
Seeking medical treatment in a foreign country
Swan songs
Unresolved cadences
Kids who eat snot
Complicating factors
Mournful gypsy love songs
Being held prisoner in an eight-foot hole for
    six months
Accidents that cause impotence
Chamberpots emptied onto the heads of
    passersby
Ambitious assistants
Isms
Insufficiently crisp apples
Butterflies shot with rifles
Escaped toddlers
Reading books just to say you read them
Obscure Renaissance humorists
The glint of a knife in the dark
Losing the habit of thought
Attacking a hornet's nest with a bat
Posture that causes chronic pain
Watching as loved ones ruin their lives
Lacking a foundation for your beliefs

Close calls

Dead maidens floating down rivers with
   flowers in their hair

Being humiliated in front of your wife and
   children

Knowing that your death wouldn't really
   bother anybody

Crumbling stone saints in cathedral niches

Being ill-suited for your profession

Humbert Humbert

Suffering caused by strangers' taste in music

Running amok

Running afoul

Realizing your life doesn't look much like the
   way you dreamed it would

Padded résumés

Feelings of sinfulness

Being cut off (while drinking)

Being cut off (while talking)

Old, grainy TV shows

Swatting flies

The strange calm of despair

Gremlins

The smell of burned-out batteries

Falling down the stairs

Children ice skating during the first thaw

Police tape

Elbow grease

Having a stick up your ass (metaphorically)

Having a stick up your ass (literally)

Pandemonium

Blood sloshing in your boots

Indian burns

Shortcuts that end up taking longer

Losing a coin toss

Fading fast

Fading slowly

Rickets

The coldest part of the night

Thinking someone won't shoot you who
actually will

When people you dislike ask you what you
think of them

Chiclets

The small urns of cremated pets

Having to walk up a broken escalator

Snipers

Looting

Plane crashes at air shows

Colostomy bags

Feeling as if the world is shrinking

Truncheoned heads

Trying to build a fire in the snow

Sunken cheeks

Woodpeckers with neck pain

Emotional starvation

Sinks stained with rust

Tossing and turning all night

Learning that your fiancé was drunk when he
proposed

Not being sure how many continents there are
Cats trained to use toilets
Not realizing you're going in circles
Kryptonite
What the earth will be like in five hundred years
Omitted umlauts
Having to identify a body in the morgue
Wearing your lucky underwear and not
    getting lucky
People who live in cardboard boxes
Days spent in bathrobes
Bowleggedness
Hurdlers who trip
Getting chlorine in your eyes
Failed attempts to erotically rip off someone's
    clothing
Cowboys shot with arrows
Trolls
Women for whom wallets are aphrodisiacs
Being told you have birthing hips
Being attacked with a shish kabob skewer
Giant squid
Sepulchres
Trying to walk across uneven ground in the
    darkness
Trying to pronounce the name of your order
    at a French restaurant
Driftwood
Nor'easters
Trying not to cry in front of someone

Trying to cry in front of someone
The unathletic children of star athletes
Odds that are not in your favor
Chefs who won't divulge their recipes
Jingle writers who dreamed of being great
    composers
Never outgrowing your baby fat
Expired prescription medications
Mansions with elevators in them
Realizing that life will go on after you die
Being able to see your breath
Scarred faces
People who say they're "pooped" when
    they're tired
Unfunny masters of ceremonies
High school teachers who hate their students
Nipple clamps
Bradypepsia, or slow digestion
Safety pins as earrings
People who refer to children as rug rats
Frozen turkeys won in bingo games
Briars
Finding your roommate going through your
    stuff
People who make sense only after four drinks
People who knock over the chessboard when
    they're losing
The monkey-eating eagle of the Philippines
Driving at suicidal speeds
Insured body parts

Broken dishwashers

Broken records

The expression: "Shit on a shingle"

Eating brains

Knuckle sandwiches

Cauterized stumps

Cultivated spiritual fatigue

Fantasies about killing your wife

Desecrated graves

Mysterious yellow clumps in the salt shaker

Knowing you could've been a contender

Uremic poisoning

Spaghetti with ketchup instead of tomato sauce

Thousand-piece puzzles

Knowing someone is humoring you

Androids

Ancient operating systems

Zima Clearmalt

Rats in fast food restaurants

Poorly dubbed foreign films

The lost Gospels

Squirrels that misjudge the distance between
branches

Abridged versions of already short books

Broken refrigerators

Stale sweat

Neighbors with meth labs

The highway to hell

Stepping on a nail

Too-tight thongs

Your last thought

Explaining adultery to children

Rain dances that don't bring rain

Studio apartments in Manhattan that cost as
  much as mansions in most countries

Breaking all ten commandments in a single day

Assisted suicide

Laws against assisted suicide

Being forced to go into hiding

Fatwa—an Islamic death sentence on infidels

The fast lane on the German autobahn, where
  speeds are so high that accidents are
  nearly always fatal

The doldrums (the feeling)

The doldrums (the equatorial zone)

The sphincter

Forests that are now neatly stacked at your
  local lumberyard

Having extra teeth

Fifty-year-olds who try to get senior discounts

Farmed salmon

Cachexia—loss of weight and muscle atrophy

Anaxagoras, who was charged with impiety
  for teaching that the moon and sun were
  physical objects and not gods

Placing fourth at the Olympic trials

People who think they're smarter than they are

Oymyakon, a town in Eastern Europe where
  a temperature of -90.4 degrees Fahrenheit
  was recorded

Twelve-foot-long earthworms

Fields irrigated by the blood of innocents

Overwatering plants

Dispossessed nations that want to be countries

Suppositories

Birds killed by helicopters

Children who consider homework optional

People who date only certain ethnicities

Summary executions

Flemish paintings of deformed children

Agamemnon's death mask

Gertrude, Hamlet's mother

Men addicted to video games

The sound of spoken German

Ugly people who try to develop winning
personalities

Plunder

Dog shit on rainy days

Bartered brides

The fact that the Supreme Court only recently
outlawed the execution of the mentally
challenged

Underage workers at meatpacking plants

Cultural variations in hygiene

Trilingual toddlers who make you look bad

Lusty old men

Kangaroo courts—mock courts set up in
violation of established legal procedure

Trying to declare your love in a foreign
language

Weak, scattered applause
Families with a history of intermarriage
Picnics that get rained out
Lou Dobbs
The population density of Monaco, which is
the highest in the world
Medieval sewer systems
Second-tier superheroes
Poor telephone etiquette
Not knowing what the plural of "moose" is
Demonically grinning monkeys
People who are a little too proud of having
friends of different ethnicities
Books with the final pages missing
Paraplegic dogs
Children left behind
Older pregnant women whose babies are
more likely to be disabled
Heiresses courted for their money
Forgotten first languages
Getting knocked out in the first round
Attempting to trace your genealogy
Teenage drug lords
The early twentieth-century custom of hair
removal by X-ray, which led to cancer
years later
The amount of shit you excrete annually
Water advertised as "made from scratch"
Settling
Power outages that last for days

Running out of wine at a dinner party
The sinking of the *Titanic*
The movie *Titanic*
Strip mining
Patients who can't get appointments for
    skin cancer treatments because their
    dermatologists are busy doing cosmetic
    procedures
Growing demand and stagnant supply
Growing supply and stagnant demand
Being gullible
Freakishly long tongues
Parochialism
Being the primary caregiver for an
    Alzheimer's patient
Ticking time bombs
Ticking time bombs used as a metaphor
Not being sure what kind of animal you're
    eating
Being afraid of a little hard work
Feeding tubes
Caligula—a Roman emperor and insane tyrant
Not dying peacefully in your sleep
Insult added to injury
Spinal cord inflammation
Bridge collapses
Bridge games
Athletes who injure themselves while
    qualifying for the Olympics and are unable
    to actually compete

Wards of the state

Lying to your spouse about your spending
    habits

Accidentally swallowing an olive pit

Studies showing that one third of Americans
    have sleep problems

Polishing the underside of the banister

Schisms

Political paralysis in Iraq

Rocket launchers

Labor shortages in Chinese factories

The butterfly effect

Chagrin

Sharks that must continually keep swimming
    or else they will drown

Teenagers who drink cough syrup to get high

Giving blood

Not giving blood and feeling bad about it

Putting your neighbor in the woodchipper

Being charged extra by a whore

Plastic surgeons who do pro bono work

Standing armies

Books that are admired but not read

Amateur prostitutes

People who hate babies

Best friends who are simply less annoying
    than everyone else

Newspapers that don't distinguish between
    global catastrophes and new gardening
    techniques

Celebrities who discuss their longing for
 privacy in nationally broadcast interviews
Choking while eating alone
The educational opportunities for African
 Americans before 1860
Nebuchadnezzar
The roughly 1 million people killed during
 construction of the Great Wall of China
Octavia, who was married to Mark Antony
 while he was having an affair with Cleopatra
Europe's Great Famine
1076, when the Roman Catholic Church began
 burning heretics
Greek fire—a burning liquid weapon used by
 the Byzantine empire
Squires whose job it was to repair knights'
 broken armor during war
Tomás de Torquemada, a prominent leader of
 the Spanish inquisition
Slow roasted humans
The Tower of London
Montezuma II—an Aztec emperor who helped
 destroy his own empire
1788, when the first tobacco advertisement
 appeared in the United States
Difficulties finding the air-raid shelter
Late-payment notices
Having to do your job and your lazy
 coworker's job
People who consider Starbucks a way of life

Waiters who always hand the check to the
    man
Horny twelve-year-old boys
Restaurants with huge portions that you
    shouldn't eat but do
The limits of etiquette
Elephant stampedes
Half-dead wolves caught in traps
Skateboarder wipeouts
Insecurely attached bungee jumpers
Flash floods
Dying just before rescue arrives
Gaping wounds
Humans caught in bear traps
Beer for breakfast
Surfers crushed by massive waves
Poorly ventilated bathrooms
People who think Barack Obama is a terrorist
Reality shows about trying to become rappers'
    personal assistants
Boy Scouts who rape people
People who rape Boy Scouts
Ugly babies in advertisements
Control-top panty hose
Politicians who consider the support of their
    corporate sponsors
Hot tears of helpless rage
Hands constantly clenched into fists
Going outside with curlers in your hair
Poets published only on refrigerator doors

Making out with someone you know your
 friend likes
Neck pain
ABBA
Factory workers who fall into meat grinders
Children traumatized by the existential
 sorrow of zoo animals
Being stuck on an opening drawbridge
Tiny broken parts of stereos
Being told to bend over
The smell of burning hair
Sex fantasies about Nancy Drew
Being unable to string your father's bow
Fraudulent disability claims
Nightmares about your boss
Aspiring writers who work as interns in
 publishing houses
Men who date girls younger than their
 wardrobes
People who pronounce Beethoven phonetically
Desperate attempts to purchase membership
 in the local country club
Defense lawyers for war criminals
Funerals exploited for political gain
Journalists who invent quotes and sources
The smug looks of people flying first class
Unknowingly funding your husband's visits to
 strip clubs
Minor dictators with delusions of global
 importance

Malfunctioning automatic toilets

Tweezers confiscated from travelers by the Department of Homeland Security

Prisoners found hanging in their cells

Former presidents who charge $100,000 for lecture appearances

Teachers who get stuck in their classroom personas

Cell phones ringing in art museums

People who drive slowly in the fast lane

Airport food

Committee meetings dominated by the least intelligent people

Presidents who constantly invoke executive privilege

T-shirts that spark lawsuits

Small boats capsized by the wakes of large boats

Finding out that your first love is now a prostitute

Sandwiches the size of a human head

Being told that you'll understand when you're older

Elderly people placed in corners at family gatherings

People who take only themselves seriously

The U.S. Merchant Marine Academy, which, according to a recent survey, has the least happy students of any college

Giving your children the same advice you ignored from your parents

The way you look before breakfast
People who grow old without growing up
Old wine that turns to vinegar
Giving up years of future happiness for a few
     moments of pleasure
Parents who can't accept that their children
     are no longer children
Feeling your age
Being caught surfing for porn at work
Talking about sex while having lunch
Making love to a mannequin
Accidentally saying "fuck" during a job
     interview
Being locked in a room with a gas leak
Appliances that break when you touch them
Boomerang-related injuries
The first snow of winter
Realizing you're too old to die young
People who think a thespian is a sort of high-
     class lesbian
Being forced to read Herman Melville
Friends who are constantly correcting your
     grammar
People who think telephones work only if they
     shout
Hangdog looks meant to induce guilt
Coworkers who fail to hide their bad moods
Automatically included tips
International vacations ruined by civil wars
Steak cooked in the microwave

Pregnant alcoholics

Pregnant kickboxers

Unexpected mud baths

Assault with a hair dryer

People who trust that their neighborhoods
are safe

Corporations that suppress studies that
suggest their products will kill you

Urinal cakes

Juggling chain saws

Men who want their wives to be both virgins
and whores

People who make all major life decisions while
drunk

Spreading contraceptive jelly on toast (a
woman actually did this and sued when
she became pregnant)

Being crushed by a vending machine you were
assaulting because it stole your money

Children who eat Silly Putty

Getting hairspray in your eyes

The roughly $43,000 a typical smoker spends
on cigarettes in a lifetime

Historically inaccurate historical dramas

Learning that an audit is not a quick hearing
check

Broken condoms that require surgical removal

Being the only person to notice your dazzling
good looks

Loud noises in dark rooms

People who become the way you treat them

Forgetting the good-bye kiss

Mistaking the servants for the children

Mistaking the children for the servants

Children who learn the hard way that a
    Halloween cape does not enable them to fly

Husbands who always take the most
    comfortable chair

People who stop making romantic gestures
    after they're married

Wives seen as unpaid housekeepers

People who automatically agree with their
    spouses

Motion-activated lights that don't respond to
    your motions

Shampoo in a baby's eyes

Novels that should have been op-ed pieces

Flaws that are charming in a lover but
    disastrous in a husband

People who listen to only good news

People who try to see the "upside" of death
    and destruction

Old grievances revisited

Refusing to give way about trifles

Constant carping

Husbands who say "that's your business"
    about their children

Buying expensive furniture for the children
    to ruin

Wives who talk to their husbands like infants

Innocent, trusting people who are taken
   advantage of until they hate everyone
Wanting to kick someone
Complaining to people who you know don't
   care
Mute reproaches
Noticing that none of your spouse's happiest
   moments involve you
Having one pair of clothes for a ten-day trip
People who don't believe in toothbrushes
Persuading yourself that your behavior is
   perfectly justified
Gastroenterologists
Expensive ingredients ruined by bad chefs
Cold mutton
Unreciprocated dinner invitations
Self-appointed members of the aristocracy
Having too many acquaintances and too few
   friends
Angry household gods
Women who insist on "spring cleaning" once
   a week
Men who hold babies as if they were bombs
Men who see monogamy as a necessary evil
Men who think monogamy is a good idea for
   women
Cowboys who brand younger cowboys as a
   hazing rite
Rural children who get attached to the pigs
   they'll soon be eating

Archaeologists who accidentally step on the mummy they're excavating

Pornography booths at the county fair

Learning that centipedes don't have one hundred legs

Freedom fries

Liberty cabbage

Swastika tattoos

Synchronized swimming

Being framed for a crime

Misspelled road signs

Unrestricted submarine warfare

Breeding in captivity

Divorces in which both parents fight to avoid custody

Suicide hotline employees

One-person family dinners

Dying before you see your enemies punished

Petty office policies

Men who tell women they should explore their sexuality

Men who tell women they should have wild anal sex

Artists who change their names to months of the year

Bitchy women at nail salons

Finding nude pictures of your husbands ex-girlfriends

Drunk conversations with supervisors at company parties

Stingy tooth fairies

Small children in large stores who can't find
    their mommies
Not being invited to your child's wedding
Parents who sue their children
People who are just sort of there
Fighting with your husband's relatives
Sadistic yoga teachers
Google-enabled stalking
Cashiers who cough on your groceries
Tall people at the movies
Failing at the morning's crossword puzzle
Questions with no right answer
Outdated train timetables
Seeing the shadow of your assailant just
    before they plunge a knife into your back
Commuters who violently scratch themselves
Roller towels in public restrooms
Being the only person who thought it was a
    costume party
Being seated next to someone you hate at a
    long dinner
People who guess your age
Great literature used as toilet paper
College English courses in which students
    talk about how books made them feel
Surprise parties for elderly people with heart
    conditions
Suspicious lipstick stains
People with December birthdays who get only
    one set of presents

Men who film their wives giving birth
Children forced to watch video footage of
their own birth
Increasingly desperate attempts to conceal
boredom
Bosses who assign intricate, lengthy tasks just
as you are going home
Bad Australian accents
Actors who always play the same part
Diets that cause weight gain
Doctors who get confused and tell the wrong
family their loved one is dead
Having no new messages
Foods ruined forever by food poisoning
Ostentatious displays of bad abstract art
Leaking waterbeds
Getting fewer presents than everyone else
College funds spent on cars
Small children with drum sets in small houses
Beautifully wrapped bad presents
Receiving a diet book as a gift
Costume weddings
Accidentally deleting important voice mails
Great white sharks
Picking a fight
Leather lizards—prostitutes at truck stops
Thinking about all the ways your life would be
better if you got a divorce
Audibly cracking joints
Just missing happy hour

Being unable to see the stars in cities
Drinking alone
Staying friends after a breakup
Not staying friends after a breakup
Sentences that end with "so . . ."
Verdigris—the green coating formed when
   metal is exposed to water
The Stasi
High crime rates in New Orleans post–
   Hurricane Katrina
Never hearing back after a job interview
Never hearing back after a first date
Thinking about the least painful way to
   commit suicide
High expectations
Low expectations
Cars driving without their lights on at night
Dogs in heat
Living in a van down by the river
Husbands who tell their wives to lose weight
Wives who tell their husbands to lose weight
People gored during the running of the bulls
Drivers who make U-turns in the middle of
   the street
People who can't think for themselves
Prank callers
Show offs
Broken zippers
Boyfriends replaced with vibrators
Wondering when your real life is going to start

Being tasered to death
Strongmen
Extradition
Mail fraud
Wire fraud
The 1994 Raboteau massacre in Haiti
Stray dogs
Straw dogs
Forensic audits
Being really good at something you hate
Being really bad at something you love
Walking on a wet floor in socks
Emoticons
Smiley faces made of thumb tacks on
communal bulletin boards
Finding mold growing on a cookie after you've
already eaten half of it
Not knowing what to say when you meet one
of your idols
The link between artificial colorings and
irritability in children
An order of Aussie Cheese Fries from
Outback Steakhouse, which contains over
2000 calories
Maltodextrin
Potassium sorbate
Propylene glycol alginate
Studies showing that nonsmokers married to
smokers have a much higher stroke risk
Emphysema

The $1.5 billion yearly cost of surgical errors
Skyrocketing rates of hospitalization for
    heart failure
Pulmonary embolism
Deep vein thrombosis
Tetrodotoxins—poisons found in puffer fish
Fatal medication errors
The 31 percent of Americans with high
    frequency hearing loss
Mild cognitive impairment
Severe cognitive impairment
Good restaurants that go under
Mortgage fraud
Being the first soldier to retreat
Houston's status as the worst recycler among
    major American cities
Dark matter
Insurance companies that won't pay for
    second opinions
Beach closings due to pollution
An eye for an eye
Having a can but no can opener
Election fraud
Runny poached eggs
The fact that high school graduation rates
    have been declining since 1980
Shifting tectonic plates
Flawed artificial joints that necessitate further
    surgery
Low consumer confidence

Biased referees

Formication—tactile hallucinations of insects crawling under the skin

Freebasing

The Brompton Cocktail—a mixture of cocaine, heroin, and alcohol once administered to terminally ill patients

Lobsters that eat each other in tanks that are too small

The 30 percent of all fatal highway crashes that are due to speeding

The "check engine" light in your car coming on

Backseat drivers

Kids fighting in the backseat while you're trying to drive

Wanderlust

Error codes

Wormholes

Penis enhancement surgery

Other women who are thinner than you

Other men who are more muscular than you

The exercise program you're planning to start . . . tomorrow

The thirty-six thousand people who die from pneumonia or influenza each year

Ischemic strokes

Atypical hyperplasia—precancerous changes in the breast

Directors' commentaries that consist of the director praising his own work

Eating a big meal and then going swimming

Epidydimal cysts—noncancerous growths on
the testicles

Ectopic pregnancy

The fact that dead chickens are washed in
chlorine before we eat them

Female suicide bombers who carry hidden
explosives past checkpoints under their
flowing garments

The Washington, D.C., riots of 1968

Qualified candidates who are turned down
from jobs because of their political views

Salim Hamdan—Osama bin Laden's former
driver

Mississippi's status as America's most obese
state

The $128 billion surplus that Bush inherited in
2001 and turned into a massive deficit

The skyrocketing demand for private cars in
China

Losing your mojo

The Mahdi Army—an anti-American Iraqi
militia

Monopolies

Snakes coiled to strike

Walking into a cactus

Tonya Harding

Celebrity Rehab with Dr. Drew

Hodgkin's lymphoma

Non-Hodgkin's lymphoma

Carbuncles
Cod liver oil
Leaving the window open when it rains
Stripped gears
Rorschach tests
Takeru Kobayashi, the competitive eating
    champion whose vigorous training led to
    an arthritic jaw
Water intoxication
Ruptured stomachs
Goody-goodies
Poorly ventilated bathrooms
The brain cells you lose with age, starting in
    your twenties
Having a word on the tip of your tongue
Dancing yourself to death in iron shoes
Thinking of the Hoover Dam when you have
    to pee
Ephemeral satisfaction
Siren songs
The KGB
Realizing you weren't listening only when
    someone asks you a question
Trench warfare
Blushing
Poachers
Wanting to have a baby but having no one to
    have it with
Animal activists who throw blood on fur coats
Trade talks breaking down

Watching stoner movies when you're not
  stoned
Hackers
Senator Ted Stevens
Fallout
Cardiac arrhythmia
Taking the low road
Elderly people with no children to take care
  of them
Accidentally filling your car's tank with jet fuel
Glowing LED lights that make it hard to sleep
  at night
The cost of living in Moscow, which is the
  highest in the world
The fact that only 1600 giant pandas are left in
  the wild
Finances after divorce
The "big one"—the catastrophic earthquake
  scientists predict will occur in California in
  the next thirty years
Studies showing that diabetic women are
  three times more likely to have children
  with birth defects
The smell of Brie cheese
Dusting
The fact that oil prices per barrel almost
  doubled between 2007 and 2008
Remotes with hard-to-find mute buttons
Velcro on shoes
Foam bras

Waiting in line for the copy machine

Lipstick that sits in the creases and lines of your lips

Cuticles

Smudging a new pedicure before it dries

Elegant dresses worn with flip-flops

Mort Hurst, who suffered a stroke after eating 38 eggs in 29 seconds

Radio announcers with beautiful voices and ugly faces

Women who name their babies after soap opera characters

Rock stars without last names

Racial profiling

Sarcastic vice principals

Shower curtains with giant fish on them

Water rings on furniture

Contagious yawns

Three-day-old shrimp

Printer ink that you can order from only specific websites

Kids' sports teams sponsored by beer companies

Someone else eating the last brownie

Discarded Coke cans found high in the remote Andes mountains

Villagers in foreign countries who offer to buy your jeans

The disappointing taste of candy you remember from childhood

Toilet paper that sticks to your shoe

Running out of antidiarrhea medication just before a formal dinner

Trying to call your in-laws by their first names for the first time

Fuzzy toilet seat covers

Eighteen-year-olds who still go trick-or-treating

Questioning your parents' political affiliation

Questioning your parents' religious affiliation

Grandfather clocks that always chime the wrong time

Cracks in your foundation

Leaky pipes

Flat pillows

People who threaten suicide to win arguments

Having an academic advisor who secretly hates you

Verbal diarrhea

Alcoholism on Native American reservations

Dogs that bite mailmen

Lumpy mattresses

Ovarian cysts

Cats that leave mouse tails in corners

The sound of a mosquito near your ear in the dark

People who are proud of being able to burp the alphabet

Living next door to a house full of college students who party every night

Learning how to make out from an article in a
    teen magazine
Rich brats forced to volunteer in soup kitchens
Realizing you were a pretty terrible parent
Dolphins with erections
Not being sure whether a title should be in
    quotes or in italics
Ex-girlfriends who want you to die
Feeling embarrassed for people who lack a
    sense of shame
First jobs
Your mother marrying one of your high
    school classmates
Summer flings that end with genital warts
Men who think that all female athletes are
    lesbians
Getting parenting advice from your mother
    that emphasizes everything she wishes
    she'd done differently with you
Advertisements that coin words like "fabulosity"
Wanting your parents' money without the
    whole parents part
Financial advisors who need advice
Financial advisors who don't follow their own
    advice
Learning the moon is not made of cheese
Judgmental gynecologists
The lack of quality hospitals in poor
    neighborhoods
Attempts to help that just make things worse

Forgetting you have an explicit screensaver
    and then opening your laptop in public
Mistaking a digression for the topic
Crying in your beer
Driving across town to a store that's closed
Dentists whose signs have pictures of
    dancing teeth
Surgeons with shaky hands
Offending a member of a motorcycle gang
Late paychecks
People who space out and just sit at green lights
Exercising when you need to shit
Being attacked by geese
Admonishments
Lousy T-shirts
Fishing in urban areas
Spending your birthday alone
Forgetting to pay bills
Difficult-to-assemble toys that your children
    never play with
People who are constantly humming tunelessly
Pranks that end in death
The food at Denny's
Troops who are considered expendable
Irreparably shattered inner peace
Casting the first stone
Atlas
Atlas Shrugged by Ayn Rand
Not being able to explain what you do for a
    living

Kings who couldn't produce a male heir

Being told: "That will be all"

Denied annulments

DES—a hormone prescribed to women
during pregnancy that led to future
reproductive problems for their children

Falling off the roof while cleaning the gutters

Being compared to an ugly actor

Being dumped because of your astrological
sign

Low self-esteem workshops

Unspoken weight loss competitions between
friends

Asking for love advice from someone who
secretly adores you and wants to ruin your
relationship

Dating a recovering sexaholic

Vomiting on nice clothes

Roommates who compulsively rearrange the
furniture

Rutting warthogs

Being told you snore

Parents disappointed with their child's gender

Men who prefer watching sports to talking to
their wives

Learning your ex committed suicide right
after you broke up

Friends lost to motherhood

Being asked to massage your grandparents'
feet

Camp musicals

Rich people who never tip

People who offer to repay large debts with beer and cigarettes

Getting caught stealing alcohol

Royal bastards

Mistaking a martini for a finger bowl

Mistaking a finger bowl for a martini

Bayoneting the wounded

The bartender's backstory

Unsolicited hugs

Finding a friend curled in the fetal position around the base of your toilet

Failed attempts to shotgun a beer

Angles from which you appear to be a different gender

People who water plants with bottled water

People who constantly quote themselves

Cynically profiting from a corporation you despise

Viragos

Alcohol-induced nationalism

Great writers who could have been more prolific if they weren't so busy drinking and having sex

Single mothers whose children ask where daddy is

Not being sure which words to capitalize

Comedians who mistake profanity for humor

Power lunches

Cafeteria workers

Corporate yoga

Moms who tell one kid they're cuter than the
other

Gondoliers who can't swim

Gondoliers who are tone deaf

Being the only child whose picture is not on
your parents' refrigerator

Naps at the bar

Yoga teachers with harsh, unsoothing voices

Brain surgeries for which you have to remain
conscious

Pocket protectors

Fashionable cracks in restaurant walls

Apprentice magicians who actually saw their
assistants in half

Breaking into a car only to realize you can't
drive a stick

Screams

Eating leftovers at every meal

Prescription drugs that differ from generics
only in their price

Having a phone number that is almost
identical to the number of an escort service

Getting stuck in traffic on your anniversary

Computers with opinions about politics

Hummingbirds trapped in the house

Funeral home employees who say: "Thank
you, come again"

The demolition of beautiful old buildings

Job applicants who are convicted felons

Cold grits

Incompetent children who inherit their parents' businesses

Men who see their professional lives as continuations of their high school football careers

Human footstools

Bosses who are former marine sergeants

Being fired for making personal photocopies

All the people you didn't know were reading your e-mail

People who think Under Armor is bulletproof

Self-expression with hackneyed catchphrases

Being told to fix your face

Recently divorced men working long hours

Knowing damaging information about murderers who know you know

Casual wearing of surgical masks

Learning someone died in a text message

Grandfathers who love to tell the story of the time they impregnated your grandmother

Tabloids that sell more copies than dozens of novels combined

Teens who emulate their pregnant teen idol role models

Bad actors turned bad directors

Fruitless debates with religious fanatics

Comedians who think their ugliness makes them funny

Employees who make more photocopies than
    decisions
Hannibal Lecter
Soda cans encrusted with rat urine
Cellular slime molds
Learning that your son was barbequed
CAFOs, or concentrated animal feeding
    operations (a fancy acronym for
    slaughterhouses)
Empty patriotic bluster on Memorial Day
Shorts in cathedrals
People who look like Modigliani paintings
Drooling while yawning
Three-day-old coffee in Styrofoam cups
The vocal chords of South American soccer
    commentators
Large families in tacky matching shirts
Countries where voting for a particular
    candidate exponentially increases your
    chance of death
Incompatible chargers
Patented colors
Novels advertised on buses
Heartworm
Ruptured spleens
Idiots with a bully pulpit
Pork chop smoothies
Ferocious mastiffs
The fact that there is a sexual position called
    the pile driver

Blight

Distraint—the seizure of personal property
    due to nonpayment
Unspecified toxic events
Relentless hawkers of cheap mementos
Owls with insomnia
Basal ganglia dysfunction
Harridans
People whose primary income is the rebate on
    recycled cans
Malfunctioning oxygen canisters while deep-
    sea diving
People who tell you "the gist" of *War and
    Peace*
Surfers eaten by sharks
Tumuli—mounds of earth and stone raised
    over graves
Hopes revised downward
Reductio ad absurdum arguments
Men nicknamed "The Widow Maker"
Companies that discontinue the pensions of
    loyal workers
Rock climbers who forget to attach the safety
    harness
Dating someone who brings out the worst in
    you
Action movies that try to be politically relevant
People on whom college is wasted
Forgetting to hide the murder weapon
High dudgeon
Companies modeled on nation-states

Nation-states modeled on companies
Whiplash from bumper cars
Not knowing when to quit
Invented statistics in advertisements
Arguments that last decades
Wanting to be someone else
The Great Man theory of history
Major life decisions based on the needs of pets
Dead showgirls in ditches outside Las Vegas
Teens shown drunk-driving carnage films in
    drivers' ed
Teens shown close-up pictures of STDs in
    health class
Forgetting dessert
Totally mundane dreams with no deeper
    meanings
Cat people
Dog people
Ordering take-out, yet again
Step-grandparents
Weekly meetings with the principal at your
    child's school
Your parents telling you to use protection
    while your date is listening
Trying to entertain hungry small children for
    hours
Hands stuck in the cookie jar
Chewing gum in hair
Running out of diapers
Stabbing yourself with your corsage

The words "please hang up and try again"
Crooked bangs
Flimsy plastic lawn chairs
Wheelbarrows with flat tires
Plastic shoes
Nostrils clogged with black soot
Getting stranded at an altitude too high for
	evacuation by helicopter
Sputum
Climbers who get within one hundred yards
	of the summit of Mount Everest and have
	to turn around
Being told to expand your skill set
Smirks
Getting caught charging personal items to the
	corporate expense account
Hair that doesn't respond to combing
Expensive medical tests that show nothing
Diamonds that aren't forever
Trying to keep a horse in a city
People who are universally beloved
Not daring to say what you think
Kathie Lee Gifford
People who try to spice up their sex lives by
	watching soap operas
Having your parents drive you to prom
Hematomas
People who skim books and then discuss them
Guided tours of former concentration camps
Not realizing when someone is talking to you

Replying to a question that wasn't asked
Replying in the wrong language
Not realizing you were on speaker phone
The last day of vacation
Puerility
Vibrators as birthday presents
Small children who trip while running joyously
    toward their mother's waiting arms
Coldplay
Mortuary school
Mistaking social tension for sexual tension
Trying to convey your life story in a few
    paragraphs
Trying to sound excited about your friends'
    lives
Imploded scuba divers
Trying to make your job sound sexy,
    impressive, and dangerous
The psychological effect of reading this entire
    book
Trying to understand string theory
Looking around you
Trying to feel sexy in long underwear
The ugliness of Abraham Lincoln
Women whose tights fail to conceal their hairy
    legs
Gratuitous high fives
Corpses dissolved with lime in bathtubs
Poor floral arrangements at funerals
Umbrellas inverted by strong winds

Rich people who emphasize their upper middle class roots

Faith healers

The English Sweating Sickness, which swept Europe between 1485 and 1552

The many many people you could never be happy with

When your toddler pours apple juice on the laptop because "it looked thirsty"

Gnats in a tornado

Xanax

People paid to wear a giant hotdog suit and dance suggestively

People whose job is to pass out fliers on the street in the summer

Bathtubs of dead baby eels

Garbage barges

Cloth diapers

Celebrities who are disappointingly short in person

Living presidents who claim as inspiration dead presidents who would have despised them

Cleaners of gas station urinals

Parents who consider their child's screaming tantrums adorable

Babies who prefer dirt to food

Meeting your future wife by dry-humping her at a frat party

Songs with one chord, played very loudly

People who hate things they have never tried

Cold Egg McMuffins

Weighing yourself ten times a day

Feeling compelled to visit your sick friends in the hospital

Poorly attended revolutions

People who think *The Waste Land* is a poem about New Jersey

Calvin Coolidge

Priests who mispronounce the name of the deceased

Older siblings who refuse to buy alcohol for their younger siblings

Out-of-service elevators

Drum sets that consist of a single bucket

Futile scratching

Pop-up bibles

Running the wrong way during a fire

Being the soldier chosen to lead the charge

The difference between listening and hearing

Human smugglers

Frighteningly efficient people

Children who come home from play dates with a newfound knowledge of sex and profanity

Wrong turns

Unhealthy anticipation of your weekly therapy session

Trying to find something nice to say about a dead person

People who view MySpace as a creative outlet

Legally Blonde the musical

Women who want their boyfriends to be more
   like John Mayer

Compulsive e-mail checking

Untalented subway musicians during morning
   rush hour

Warm Frappuccinos

Wiping barbeque sauce off your husband's face

Friends who always ask for relationship
   advice and never give it back

Babysitting a young child who insists on
   talking about how babies are made

People who think makeup makes them look
   better when it doesn't

Women who don't consider their husbands
   their friends

Having multiple nightmares in one night

Senior citizens retiring in college towns

Working at a sleepaway camp and not liking
   any of the other counselors

Failed extortion attempts

Drag queens who have better legs than your
   girlfriend

Drag queens who are better in bed then your
   girlfriend

Holier-than-thou people who really are holier
   than you

Crocodile-skin accessories

Ideologies with no foundation in reality

Fights that resume as soon as you leave
   couples' counseling

Awkwardly rhymed verse

Health food that makes you fart

Essays with puns in the title

Not knowing which countercultural
movement is chic right now

Partial erections

Dying street dogs that are better groomed
than your boyfriend

People who try to "play" champagne flutes

A spelling system completely at odds with
modern pronunciation

Tropical diseases

Misuse of the semicolon

People who won't have sex with you, even if
you pay

Countries with currency more colorful than ours

Immigrants who speak your language better
than you do

Having the wrong limb amputated

The world's richest men ignoring the poverty
around them

When your favorite band's concert gets
rained out

Religions that don't allow marriage to animals

Noisy crickets

Glorious art that makes you realize how
fucked you are

Poorly cooked roadkill

The poverty of words

Banks open only when everyone is at work

Cognitive dissonance

White subtitles in black-and-white movies

ATM transaction fees

Not having peripheral vision while wearing glasses

Attractive people who wear baggy clothes

Having to read Old English poems in the original

Impenetrable academic writing supported by large grants

The porn store clerk knowing your name

Recent Woody Allen films

The difficulty of owning a restaurant

People who get everything handed to them on a silver platter

Your global multimedia empire's lackluster profits this quarter

Wi-Fi hotspots that are actually cold

The Victorian novel

Sentences that begin with the words: "When I was your age"

Gun-toting psychopaths, especially when they run countries

Shakespeare's failure to attain physical immortality through his verse

Traveler's diarrhea when you haven't left home

The price of condoms

Antibacterial soap

Children who grow up to be as stupid as their parents

Getting flowers and syphilis for Valentine's Day
The job prospects of an aging dominatrix
When your roommates throw each other
  birthday parties and don't throw one for you
Hearing ambulance sirens during your wedding
Adult cartoons
Babies with milk allergies
Wanting kids when your husband doesn't
Wanting kids when your wife doesn't
Being the last one with your family name
Getting so drunk on a booze cruise that you
  decide to go swimming in a filthy harbor
Mohels with shaky hands
Getting stung by a jellyfish
The characters in porn films
Animals with jars stuck on their heads
Being cross-eyed
Walking into a spiderweb
Flaneurs
Accidents with electric drills
Trying to get a table at a hot new restaurant
Being told you can't do something
Having to change your name because you're
  being stalked
Margaret Seltzer, who wrote a memoir about
  LA gang life that turned out to be fictional
Peeling skin post-sunburn
Trying to find a new tenant
Oxybenzone—a potentially toxic ingredient in
  sunscreen

Pigeon droppings on city sidewalks
The magazine selection in doctors' offices
Thin eyelashes
Fat fingers
IVs that won't go in
Stripped screws
Leaky paint sprayers
Getting your privates shaved at the hospital
Picking someone up from the airport after
    midnight
Getting an eye infection from old mascara
Flat soda
Spilling tomato juice on a white carpet
Numbness after Novocain
The amount of packaging involved in frozen
    dinners
Forgetting the time difference and calling
    your grandmother after 11:00 P.M.
Finding *Playboy* magazines under your uncle's
    mattress
Plastic furniture
Black, swollen tongues
Having to make your own birthday cake
Your house getting appraised at much less
    than you thought it was worth
Bra straps that dig into your shoulders
Raccoons eating all the koi in your koi pond
Combs with broken teeth
Dry, crusty elbows
Forgetting the emergency brake on a steep hill

Having someone pretend to love you in order
to make someone else jealous

Flapping shoe soles

Eyebrows that resemble caterpillars

Your boyfriend finding your eighth grade
school picture

Barflies

Musty smelling attic fans

Pleated khakis

Not understanding your computer's instructions

Elephants that escape from the circus and
trample people

Fancy hotels with bedbugs

Motel fires

Realizing that autumn is over

Living next door to a woman who screams
constantly at her children

Ant farms

Grandparents who tell you the same stories
every time you see them

Starving artists who wish they'd gone to law
school

Wealthy lawyers who wish they'd gone to art
school

Your mom having better legs than you

Your dad being able to beat you up

Christmas ball earrings

Finding out that your favorite tree is diseased
and has to be cut down

Finding a bloated corpse while scuba diving

Not being sure whose foot you're touching
    under the table
Baboon attacks
Dusty closets
Flesh-eating plants
Blow jobs that just don't end
Double-edged swords
Sharing a bathroom with people who never
    clean it
Spending more hours each week with your
    coworkers than your spouse
Wolves in sheep's clothing
Partitioned kingdoms
Running into your teacher while either or both
    of you are drunk
Hopes crushed with a single word
Hanging out at the mall, hoping to get laid
Being asked what took you so long in the
    bathroom
The smell of other people's popcorn
Parents who consider their children a source
    of unpaid labor
Relationships that begin in closets and end in
    court
Movies referred to as "the comedy event of
    the season"
Sporks
Computers from the '80s
Teachers who try to be friends with their
    students

Learning your grandparents loved anal sex
Being born after the good old days
Having all the right lottery numbers but one
Being tied to the bed and then forgotten
History
Teeth smashed with rifle butts
Empty canteens on long marches
Hyperbolic blurbs on the backs of books
Rolling out of bed in your sleep
Kids who spend more time each week with
their computers than their friends
Soggy sandwiches
Diet soda
Magazine articles that promise that you can
eat more and lose weight
Drinking caffeine before bed
All the romantic things you used to do
together
Trying to keep your head above water
Burying your parents
Burying your children
Military curfews
Getting a voice mail from Alec Baldwin
Walking barefoot on rocky roads
Subsistence farming
People who write "have a good summer" in
your yearbook
C & D Distributors, the parts supply firm that
charged the U.S. military $293,451 for
shipping an 89 cent washer to a base

Goatees Deathwatches
Needing a new transmission
Knowing all the words to "Ice Ice Baby"
The Montauk Monster
The Tulip Mania of 1636, the first significant
    speculative bubble
Taking the nonscenic route
Sanctions
MTV
Mudslinging
Saying "I love you" too soon
The word "chunky"
The narrowing space between your upper
    thighs
Learning famous German novelists were once
    members of the Hitler Youth
Completely humorless coworkers
Coworkers who are constantly making bad
    jokes
Being a major character in someone else's
    psychodrama
Dave Matthews
Siege towers
Soldiers who fall asleep on duty
Doormen who fall asleep on duty
Tie dye
Finally figuring out who you are and realizing
    you don't like it
Mean girls
People who wear knit hats in summer

Being on the chopping block
Damp underarms
Dull razor blades
Kids who would rather play Guitar Hero than
    learn to play guitar
Water moccasins
Private clubs
Blackheads
Whiteheads
Xanadu
The clutch of greed
Failed utopias
Alberto Gonzales
Learning that your father has killed people
Hair metal
Dolphins, the only animals besides humans
    that commit suicide
Lost dog posters
Thick Cockney accents
Houses decorated with somber portraits of
    dead ancestors
Exchanges of sentence fragments that pass
    for conversation
Being trapped in a sewer
Learning what your employees really think
    of you
Disliking people who witness your humiliation
Being addressed as "ma'am"
When your parent is your teacher
The hero in Visconti's *The Bicycle Thief*

Returning from a long war to find your wife
    besieged by suitors
Snarling toddlers
Invalids who look grateful when spoken to
Writers who don't waste time reading
The death of haberdashery as an apprenticed
    craft
The Village of Tiger Widows, full of women
    whose husbands were killed by tigers
Comic book conventions
The marriage prospects of 18th-century
    British peasants
Heterosexual flight attendants
Being your husband's secretary
Chaucer's use of meter
Weekly breakfast dates with elderly women
Critics who delight in savagely cruel reviews
Artistic impulses exhausted by marriage
Adults who ask the waiter which dish is
    yummiest
The lack of fact-checkers for the Bible
Pubic hair in keyboards
Old people boasting about their sexual
    prowess
Mormon temples that look like spaceships
Movies designed to make men feel that their
    penises are large
Mothers too fat to lift their children
Vacations within a mile radius of home
Missing key body parts

Memoirs about being a slut
Parents who give their kids cash prizes for
    weight loss
Siblings who are cuter than you are
Celebrity meltdowns
Things that go bump in the night
People who consider ass-licking a spiritual
    experience
Erik Prince, CEO of Blackwater
Getting screened at airports because you
    share a name with a known terrorist
A sea of tears
Getting pulled over for driving too slow
Ketamine
Once-famous bands that now play state fairs
Kitty Genovese, who was stabbed to death
    while multiple bystanders did nothing
The Cretaceous-Tertiary Meteorite, which
    may have wiped out the dinosaurs
Wildebeests
Too much information
The persistent rumor that Catherine the Great
    died while having sex with a stallion
Weapons of mass destruction
Unfathomable darkness
Happiness

ACKNOWLEDGMENTS

There are so many despicable, depressing human beings who made this book possible that we can't thank them all here. But there are a few we'd like to thank personally. We'd like to give a shout out to Dante, Asha, Yenu, and Tadu, who provided much-needed breaks from all the sorrow. We'd like to thank Rebecca and Brett, who literally made the book possible (in the best possible way). We'd also like to thank our agent, Scott Mendel, for all his hard work. And finally, we'd like to thank all of our friends who shared things from their own miserable lives.

Photo by Michelle Maloy Dillon

LIA ROMEO is an award-winning comic playwright who has worked as a P.R. account executive, a receptionist, and a Subway sandwich artist, all of which have equipped her superbly for writing this book.

NICK ROMEO is a fiction writer and public intellectual of whom the public is not yet aware. His current day job has sunk him into a deep malaise, which he has little hope of ever escaping.